CANADA: WHAT IT IS, WHAT IT CAN BE

CANADA

WHAT IT IS, WHAT IT CAN BE

Roger Martin & James Milway

With a foreword by **Michael Porter**

UNIVERSITY OF TORONTO PRESS
Toronto Buffalo London

© Institute for Competitiveness & Prosperity 2012
Rotman-UTP Publishing
University of Toronto Press
Toronto Buffalo London
www.utppublishing.com
Printed in Canada

ISBN 978-1-4426-4465-6

Printed on acid-free, 100% post-consumer recycled paper with
vegetable-based inks.

Library and Archives Canada Cataloguing in Publication

Martin, Roger L.
Canada : what it is, what it can be / Roger Martin & James Milway.

Includes bibliographical references and index.
ISBN 978-1-4426-4465-6

1. Labor productivity – Canada.   2. Competition – Canada.   3. Economic
development – Canada.   4. Canada – Economic policy.   5. Economic
forecasting – Canada.   I. Milway, James, 1951–   II. Title.

HC120.L3M37 2012   331.11'80971   C2012-900877-X

University of Toronto Press acknowledges the financial assistance to its
publishing program of the Canada Council for the Arts and the Ontario
Arts Council.

 Canada Council   Conseil des Arts
for the Arts   du Canada

 ONTARIO ARTS COUNCIL
CONSEIL DES ARTS DE L'ONTARIO

University of Toronto Press acknowledges the financial support of the
Government of Canada through the Canada Book Fund for its publishing
activities.

CONTENTS

FOREWORD

In 1990–1 Roger Martin, John Armstrong, and I collaborated on an initiative to re-examine Canadian competitiveness called *Canada at the Crossroads*. The study examined Canada's political, legal, and macroeconomic context, the quality of its microeconomic business environment, and the sophistication of operations and strategy in Canadian-based businesses.

Though Canada had traditionally enjoyed economic prosperity and a high standard of living on the basis of its rich natural-resource endowments, we saw changes on the horizon. Basing a nation's competitive advantage in commodities was risky. The federal deficit was unsustainably high, as were taxes, especially those on business investment. Firms faced little local competition, little pressure from customers, and infrastructure constraints. Too many firms seemed content to compete in Canada alone, with little emphasis on the global marketplace. All of this discouraged investment and innovation and thus put Canada's future prosperity at risk.

Out of *Canada at the Crossroads* came controversy, a spirited dialogue in Canada, and many changes in both policy and business, which has continued. The project also led over time to the formation of the Institute for Competitiveness and Prosperity, which has become a central and valued voice in the Canadian competitiveness dialogue.

Twenty years later, much has changed in Canada. Intensification of competition, the increasing globalization of companies, and a sounder macroeconomic foundation mean that Canada now finds itself in a far better position. Canada's fiscal situation is better than that of most other developed economies, unemployment is relatively low, and natural resources are again in high demand at least for now. Wilfrid Laurier once famously claimed that the twentieth century would belong to Canada. As it turns out, it didn't. But might the twenty-first?

Roger Martin and his colleague Jim Milway ask that very question in this new work. Building on a decade of impressive work at the Institute for Competitiveness and Prosperity, Martin and Milway provide a fact-based diagnosis, in readable and understandable terms, of Canada's innovation challenges, exposing some myths in the public discourse along the way. They offer practical recommendations on how Canada can achieve its prosperity potential – extending and adding to the recommendations we first made twenty years ago. Their advice for supporting innovation in the tax system, opening trade widely, and better recognizing the importance of management talent and sophisticated business strategy for innovation all resonate well beyond Canada's borders. This work makes a valuable contribution to the global body of knowledge on competitiveness and prosperity, which has been a major research interest of mine for the past three decades.

Roger and Jim identify Canada's great economic strengths, as well as its challenges. Importantly, they urge Canadians to aim for more. Only if Canadians make it a priority to achieve their prosperity potential will Canada become all that it can be.

Michael E. Porter
Bishop William Lawrence University Professor
Harvard Business School

CANADA: WHAT IT IS, WHAT IT CAN BE

PROLOGUE

Canadians are proud of their country and rightly so. Our ancestors and our own generation have built one of the most prosperous economies in the world. In fact, there are very few other countries that have achieved the economic success we have. This achievement is not just a product of the current worldwide economic turmoil, during which other countries have fallen back relative to us. It is a long-standing success. Canadians have a track record of providing economic opportunity for our citizens and for countless immigrants establishing a new life for themselves and their children.

Materially, Canadians are better off than most of the world's population. As we'll see, compared to most other developed economies, our incomes are high. Our economy creates jobs better than the rest. We have many companies – lots more than people realize – that are global leaders in their industries. We have health-care and education systems that are the envy of the world. And, even in non-material terms, we're near the top. Survey after survey shows we are a happy lot. We are justifiably proud of the cultural mosaic that is Canada. Diversity has led to problems elsewhere, but it is a source of strength in our country.

Politicians through the decades in Canada have asked rhetorically: Is there any other province or country you would rather live in? We respond with a heartfelt and emphatic 'No, this is absolutely the best place in the world.'

And yet Canada can do so much better. Economically, we're adrift. We run the risk of being left behind over the long term as developing economies catch up with the developed world. In the not-too-distant future, countries like Brazil or India or China could be the driving force behind advances in innovation, design, styles – and living standards. On our current trajectory, Canada could become yesterday's economy, with lots of old wealth and a great place to visit for the scenery – but not the place where the economic action is leading to prosperity.

Apart from the possible future threat from developing economies, we're concerned that we are coming up short against our developed-economy peers. We've been falling farther behind the United States in competitiveness and prosperity over the last few decades. Every year our economy has trailed the U.S. economy a little more, so that a fairly wide prosperity gap has emerged – even though the United States has been mired in a severe economic slump since the financial crisis of 2007–8.

Readers may wonder at this point why we are considering the United States as a benchmark. The answer is that we think the U.S. performance is useful for tracking and comparing our performance. While Canada's population is much smaller than that of the United States, we have a similar history and background, political institutions, attitudes, geography, and economic structure. And we'll see that, not too long ago, our economy performed much the same way. So comparing the Canadian and American economies is reasonable.

In this book, we'll elaborate on what we mean by the term 'prosperity gap,' and we'll show how we've fallen behind. We'll also show that this has real consequences for the average Canadian today. We'll meet the Schmidt family, whose situations and experiences represent those of other Canadians. And we'll demonstrate that, in critical areas of economic performance, we underachieve in comparison not just with the United States but also with most other developed economies.

Specifically, the Canadian economy is underperforming because productivity is lower here than it is in the United States as well as Belgium,

France, Germany, Italy, and the Netherlands. To describe the concern, we'll explain what 'productivity' is and why it matters.

Simply put, productivity measures how much value we create with a given amount of work effort. Think of two factories producing tires. Each has the same number of workers with the same work week. So the two factories are drawing on the same amount of work effort. But Factory A generates a lot more value from its production than Factory B. After both factories have sold the tires they produced and paid for their outside purchases like rubber, other raw materials, and electricity, Factory A has made more money. From these funds created by the value added to raw materials, Factory A pays wages and retains profits for future investment and dividends for the owners.

Factory A is more productive. It uses the same amount of work effort and creates more value. Three questions naturally follow: Why is it more productive? What is the benefit of this added productivity? And so what?

As we'll see, productivity is the result of more efficient operations or more innovation or both. Factory A could have a better flow of production through its plant, so that it simply produces more tires in a day than Factory B. Or it could have invested in better machinery. Perhaps the workers at Factory A are more skilled, so that fewer defects are produced, or the workers have made suggestions on how to improve operations. Perhaps Factory A's owners have designed a better tire – so they can charge a higher price for the ones they produce. Their credit department might be more adept at identifying customers who might not pay their bills, so they lose less in bad debts.

It's probably clear how Factory A benefits. Profits are higher so that owners can earn a decent return and invest for future productivity. Workers likely earn more – higher wages are the most direct effect of higher productivity. Factory A is more likely to gain new business – perhaps at the expense of Factory B – and expand. Factory A is probably a more desirable place to work for both hourly workers and managers. No doubt, the local economic development office and politicians much prefer having Factory A in their city.

Broaden this story to a country's economy. A country whose businesses are more productive will pay higher wages and be more innovative. It will create more opportunity for its youth. Its standard of living will be higher.

Canada is like Factory B. Our economy has lower productivity than most other advanced countries' economies. Our businesses create less value per hour worked than their counterparts elsewhere. This productivity gap is the source of our prosperity gap. Canada is near the top in total number of hours worked per capita, but the value Canadians create when they work lags results in other countries. This is important because our lower productivity means our standard of living is not as high as it could be. Our families could have more disposable income, our companies could invest more in their businesses, and our governments could invest more in social and investment programs without raising tax rates.

In his groundbreaking 1990 book, *The Competitive Advantage of Nations*, Michael Porter concluded that 'a nation's standard of living is determined by the productivity of its economy ... Productivity allows a nation to support high wages, a strong currency, and attractive returns to capital – and with them a high standard of living.' Similarly, in his 1997 book, *The Age of Diminished Expectations*, Nobel Laureate Paul Krugman summed up the importance of productivity nicely: 'Productivity isn't everything, but in the long run it is almost everything. A country's ability to improve its standard of living over time depends almost entirely on its ability to raise its output per worker.'

If we want Canada to achieve its prosperity potential, Canadians have to achieve our productivity potential – and we see no fundamental reason why Canada has to accept being a productivity laggard. We'll review the many reasons for our productivity deficit. Some of the more important factors are our lower levels of education versus our U.S. counterparts, especially among our managers; our businesses' lower rates of investment in technology and research and development (R&D); our lack of competitive pressure to encourage more strategies of innovation from our businesses; and our greater propensity for living in non-metropolitan regions.

Our governments need to focus more of their spending on investing for future prosperity and less on consuming current prosperity. And, as Canadians, we need to increase our investments in education, since workers' and managers' skills will be a defining element of success; in fact, they already are and we're behind. We have to be bold and creative in teaching innovation skills to our youth, because – contrary to some beliefs – innovation is a skill that can be learned.

We have to determine how best to encourage our businesses to develop more innovative strategies and to invest in R&D and technology to support these strategies. We can accomplish this by providing businesses with more educated workers and managers. But we can also apply pressure to them by expanding international trade. At the same time, we can improve our policies to reduce poverty. From an economic perspective, we have to draw on as many of our people as possible to expand the pie. It is an economic and social tragedy when some of our citizens are not helping create value and are not sharing in the benefits of our efforts.

By pursuing initiatives like these and others, Canada can become a more productive and innovative nation. Our aim should be to close the prosperity gap with the United States.

We recognize that this will be a slow climb, lasting a decade or more. And we do not propose a single policy that will create a Canadian productivity miracle. Instead, we have several recommendations that, taken together, will put us on to a path that makes others around the world ask: 'What's going on in Canada? How did it become a hotbed of innovation, economic progress, and prosperity?'

As great as Canada is, this book is about what Canada can be. Our overall theme is that Canadians are not realizing their full economic potential, as evidenced in the growing gap in Gross Domestic Product (GDP) per capita between Canada and the United States. The average family would benefit a lot if Canada fulfilled its potential.Closing the GDP per capita gap would result in an increase of $12,000 in annual after-tax disposable income for each Canadian household (Exhibit 1). And closing the prosperity gap would generate an additional $105 billion in tax revenues for all three levels of government across the country.

Exhibit 1 **Canadian families would have higher living standards if the prosperity gap were closed**

Average annual household spending in Canada (C$ 2010)

Closing the prosperity gap
$12,000 more personal disposable income per household

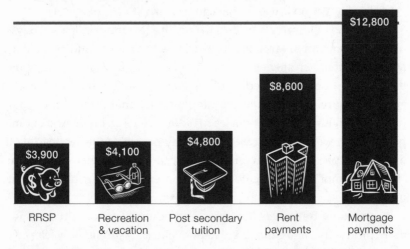

RRSP	Recreation & vacation	Post secondary tuition	Rent payments	Mortgage payments
$3,900	$4,100	$4,800	$8,600	$12,800

Note: Among Canadians with some spending in these categories; 2009 results restated to 2010 dollars.
Source: Institute for Competitiveness & Prosperity analysis based on data from Statistics Canada, *Spending Patterns in Canada 2009*.

This would increase Canadians' overall well-being and support higher spending on education, health care, and social programs.

In this book, we'll be urging Canadians to work at closing the prosperity gap that we have identified. We'll describe what the prosperity gap is and review how it has been widening over the last three decades. We'll explain why it matters to all Canadians. And we'll set out recommendations for how we can close the gap.

First, we need to be determined to close the gap, rather than be complacent that the gap doesn't matter. We all need to find ways to innovate and work smarter so that Canadians are the most productive people in the world. We'll need to invest in education and productivity-enhancing technologies. And we'll need market and governance structures that encourage innovation and risk taking rather than preserving the status quo.

No doubt the promise of higher incomes and better government services ought to be compelling for Canadians. But our book is about more than improving material comforts. We think that closing the productivity gap is worthwhile to achieve our full innovation potential as Canadians. To do otherwise would be a waste and a shame. Our parents invested in us and our country. We owe it to our children to do likewise. No other society has the opportunity that we do here in Canada at the outset of the twenty-first century.

Meet the Schmidts

Throughout the book, we follow the Schmidt family as they experience the economy on an as-it-is trajectory and on an as-it-can-be trajectory.

Michael and Maria Schmidt are a typical Canadian couple. They recently observed two significant milestones. They celebrated their thirtieth wedding anniversary. And, with a sigh of relief, two years ago they finally paid off the mortgage on their three-bedroom brick bungalow in Burlington, Ontario, to which they have added a sun porch and an outdoor pool. They've been in this house for about fifteen years. Michael is on the GO train every morning to commute to his job in downtown Toronto.

Michael, fifty-four, is a manager of data integrity for Internet and mobile banking at one of Canada's large banks. Including his bonus, he earned just over $100,000 last year. He received his bachelor's degree in English at the University of Western Ontario. He grew up in Windsor and was the first in his family to pursue post-secondary education, joining the bank upon graduation. For the first ten years, he moved around the country, working at retail and commercial branches. Along the way, he found that he was more and more interested in the banks' computer systems and learned as much as he could through bank programs and local colleges. He made the switch into the systems department and has moved steadily through the ranks since then.

His wife, Maria, is fifty-two and teaches Grade 7 in Burlington. She grew up in London and attended Western so that she could live at home. That's where she and Michael met. They married once Michael had settled in at his first management position at the bank, as an assistant manager in Cornwall, Ontario. Maria left teaching to raise their family and was able to rejoin the profession after their youngest child was in high school. She found it much easier to get a teaching job once her family had stopped relocating and settled in Burlington.

Michael's father had a traditional assembly-line job in the automobile industry and his mother stayed at home. His father's family were farmers in Grey County, near the Bruce peninsula in Ontario. His mother's family had worked in the forestry industry near East Harrington, Quebec, along the Ontario border about an hour east of Ottawa.

Maria's family immigrated from Orvieto in Umbria, Italy, to Canada when she was three years old. Like most Italian immigrants at the time, Maria's father spoke no English. He found a job in construction when he got to Canada, and her mother stayed at home. She took various jobs like housecleaning and babysitting to help make ends meet. Like Michael, Maria was the first in her family to go to university.

Michael and Maria have three children: Sandra, twenty-seven, is a single mother who is working and finishing her university education; Kevin, twenty-five, is just starting out as an investment banker; and Louise, eighteen, is just completing high school and is about to go to university.

We'll learn more about the Schmidts and how they live in the economy, since they personify many of the trends we will be discussing:

- The Canadian economy is much less insulated than it was when Michael and Maria grew up and has become even more global since Sandra, Kevin, and Louise were children; it will only get more so. But the world isn't getting flatter, it's getting spikier.
- Whereas plentiful resources like forests and mines were once critical to Canada's success, our future prosperity will depend on our ability to innovate products, services, and processes; Canadians every-

where – in the private and public sector, young and old, physical workers, service workers, and knowledge workers – will need to gain skills to innovate.

- The imperative for more education continues to grow. The Schmidt children will likely move through many different careers, much more so than their parents or grandparents. They will need a solid base of knowledge and skills, but they will also have to upgrade their skills constantly. With the advance of globalization and technology, fewer jobs are for life and skills atrophy.

The Book's Plan

The book is organized in three parts. In Part One we set out Canada's economic performance over the last decades, with a focus on the competitiveness of our people and businesses. We conclude that we work more than most others in the developed world, but are less productive and innovative. In Part Two we discuss the three drivers of productivity and innovation – where we live and work, how we compete, and how we invest – and how Canada fares on each. Our economic system is 'tuned' to be in complete equilibrium. Like a car, its various parts are in sync with each other – businesses compete at a level demanded by their customers and competitors, skills are adequate to compete at the current level, education policy responds to today's needs for skills, and so on. Yet, even so, the economy is not performing at its best. That will come when we do what's necessary to elevate performance, when all elements in the economy are tuned to hum along – like a high-performance car.

We're not there yet. Canada's economy performs well up to a point. But then it stops. Canadians invest to the level required for our firms to be competitive in our home market. But that level is below what we see in a more sophisticated economy, like that of the United States. We educate ourselves to achieve excellent high school graduation rates but fall behind the U.S. performance in the percentage of our people earning university bachelor degrees and are even farther behind in graduate degrees. Our businesses invest adequately in buildings and basic machinery, but fall behind in investments in technology. Our governments invest significantly in basic research, but our business R&D trails. We reward creativity and other important skills. But we reward these skills less than the United States.

We have a lower level of sophistication that is consistent with our lower level of competitive intensity in Canada. Our businesses invest only what they need to; they pay wage levels necessary to retain talent. Our consumers are less demanding than Europeans, for example, who want and get high-quality products. This lower level of sophistication means lower rates of innovation, lower productivity, and lower wages. And this lower tuning of our economy is what's holding us back from achieving our prosperity potential.

In Part Three we turn to the prescription for getting us to a new equilibrium – to 'tune' our economy to a higher level of sophistication. We'll recommend changes in tax policy and in our approach to innovation, we'll look at the importance of strong management, and we'll see why Canada needs even more international trade. We'll present twelve specific and innovative recommendations to make Canada what it can be.

PART ONE

Working More But Not Smarter

Canada is one of the most prosperous countries in the world. But our success will be sustainable only if we increase our productivity and innovation. Our advantage is that Canadians are very successful at creating and filling jobs. But we're not so skilled at innovation. In the long term, as our demographics shift, our worker advantage will become less significant; and, as emerging economies become more and more sophisticated, our innovation advantage will become more tenuous.

In chapter 1 we define the terms competitiveness and prosperity and show why doing well in these areas is important for all Canadians.

In chapter 2 we review the basis for prosperity – how much people work and how much value they create when they work. Our prosperity growth in Canada has been the result of success in both factors. Compared to most other developed economies, Canada excels in the first factor, work effort. But we are laggards in the second, productivity.

In chapter 3 we elaborate on our productivity challenge in Canada. We try to explain what productivity means and why it matters to the average Canadian. And we conclude that productivity and innovation are inextricably linked – indeed, close to being synonymous.

1 What Are Competitiveness and Prosperity?

Competitiveness and prosperity are the watchwords of a country's ability to thrive in the global economy. As globalization embraces many more countries, Canada cannot be complacent about the challenges to its position as one of the world's most prosperous nations. In fact, we face an imperative to be more innovative and to raise our prosperity to maintain our top ranking. Not realizing our prosperity potential has negative consequences for all Canadians.

Competitiveness Is How We Create Economic Value

A nation's competitiveness is a function of its ability to create economic value from natural, physical, and human resources in a way that is uniquely advantageous to the nation. Three elements are critical – *resources*, ability to *add value* to these resources, and success in meeting *rivalry* from other countries and regions.

Natural, Physical, and Human Resources Are the Foundation of Competitiveness

Investments in developing our natural, physical, and human resources are a necessary and ongoing element of competitiveness. And, as economies develop, the importance of these three types of resources shifts.

Natural resources, such as ports, forests, or mineral deposits, are often the first foundation of an economy. At Canada's discovery and early days in the 1500s and 1600s, the most important natural resources were fisheries and harbours in Atlantic Canada, furs in Quebec and beyond, and forests in Ontario and Quebec. In the 1700s and 1800s, our vast agricultural advantages in western Canada and plentiful mineral resources in Ontario and Quebec were important to our economic growth. In the 1900s, physical resources like manufacturing facilities and infrastructure became more important. Our natural water resources at Niagara and Churchill Falls, to name a couple, were important sources of low-cost power. Although a small market, Canada's manufacturing prowess was an important contributor to its economic growth. Our infrastructure, our labour force, and our proximity to the U.S. market gave us a manufacturing edge that we capitalized on.

We are now in the era when human resources matter most. Innovation and creativity are the major sources of economic value. More and more of our people work in sophisticated service industries, like financial institutions and telecommunications firms, where brainpower and social-intelligence skills – such as being able to understand others, work in teams, and persuade others – are critical to Canada's economic advantage.

Adding Value to These resources Is the Key to Economic Success

Having a latent strength in any resource is necessary, but not sufficient. People and organizations need to develop these resources to transform them into products and services that people will buy. Early on in Canada's history, our fishers, hunters, foresters, and farmers drew on our natural resources to deliver fish, furs, lumber, and wheat to domestic and international markets. The human effort expended in this process was decisive. For example, the large tracts of land in western Canada lay fallow until humans tilled the soil, scattered seeds, and gathered up the harvest. In economic terms, these are value-adding activities.

As Canada became a manufacturing nation, the process of adding value grew more complex and interconnected. We added value to minerals by making and rolling steel; we then added value to these steel rolls by manufacturing automobiles and other goods. Large organizations were necessary to raise financial capital, to plan the facilities and the work effort, and to find markets for our products.

We are still adding value to our endowment of natural and physical resources to create economic value for Canada. But now we have a greater supply of what is called human capital – the know-how individuals and organizations gain through formal education and years of experience. Individuals and organizations are major sources of value added, and public investments in education, health care, and infrastructure are important contributors. University-educated designers, for example, are helping create products and software that can be used at home and around the world to help manufacturing facilities produce more or for people to live better lives. We're all familiar with the BlackBerry story. But we have examples of lesser-known Canadian firms competing internationally – for example, Husky Injection Moulding in plastics moulding, Magna in automotive parts, Patriot Forge in manufacturing processes for forging metal, and Keilhauer Industries in ergonomically designed office furniture.

As we measure and monitor Canada's competitiveness and prosperity, we use GDP per capita as the summary measure of success. GDP represents the value added to our endowed base of natural, physical, and human resources. It is the sum of all the value-added processes that occur across our economy.

At its most basic level, 'value' is the worth that the customers assign to a product or service – what they are willing to pay. As we have seen, 'added' refers to the increase in value from a process, or by an organization, as a product or service moves toward its final stage. More formally, 'value added' is the worth of something above and beyond the value of the intermediate inputs used in the process that created it.

In our tire-factory example, a firm purchases raw materials, other supplies, services, and land and buildings to enable it to carry out its business. The owners and workers in the firm develop the process for

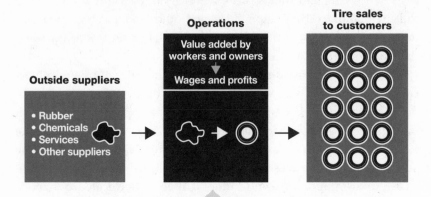

Exhibit 2 **Tire-factory workers and owners add value to earn wages and profits**

Operations

Tire sales to customers

Value added by workers and owners
▼
Wages and profits

Outside suppliers

- Rubber
- Chemicals
- Services
- Other suppliers

Value added is higher when:
- Better products and services are in demand by customers
- Workers are skilled and motivated
- Managers are effective in operations, performance, and people skills
- Operations benefit from advanced technology
- Support systems are effective

Source: Institute for Competitiveness & Prosperity.

converting the purchased inputs into output that customers pay for. The difference between what customers pay for the outputs and what the firm pays to outsiders for the inputs is the 'value added' by the firm. Value added pays wages to workers and profits to owners (Exhibit 2). The total value added divided by the number of labour hours is referred to as 'labour productivity.' There are other ways to calculate productivity – for example, the productivity of the capital invested – but our focus is on labour productivity.

Value added can be increased by developing better operating processes to convert the purchased inputs to outputs. Or it can be increased by creating a better product or service that customers pay a premium for.

As products and services are created, different people and organizations along the way add value at every step. A sandwich bought in a restaurant begins with a farmer sowing and harvesting grain. The value added at this early stage is the selling price of the grain minus the cost of the seeds, fertilizer, and machine power required in the agricultural process. The farmer's wages and profit are equal to the value added at that stage. Eventually, when a bakery sells the bread, the sale price of the bread minus the price paid for the grain and other inputs is the value added at this stage. In the case of a sandwich, this process operates in parallel for the production of sliced meat, cheese, and mustard, for example. Included in the value added is the cost of the restaurant and its staff. They, too, have a measurable value that is added to the cost of the final sandwich, minus its many inputs.

Value added at each stage is shared between the worker and the business owner – higher value added means higher wages and profits. This process of adding value continues until a final good or service is produced and provided to the end consumer. The total value added throughout the production chain is the sum of the value added in each of the individual processes.

Value added is an important concept for understanding innovation and productivity issues. Companies with higher value-added processes are likely to produce more innovative and more complex products – and this means higher productivity. Their products and processes are also more defensible in the global marketplace, making the home country more competitive. The advent of globalization has seen the movement of low value-added processes to lower-wage countries like China and India.[1] Advanced economies with high-skilled, high-wage workers like Canada will not thrive by attempting to hang on to these low value-added activities.

Innovation is a key driver of higher value added. One type of innovation occurs when a business reorganizes work flow or changes a facility's layout to make production processes run smoother, thereby lowering costs while delivering the same product or service to its customers. Another type is the redesign of an existing product or service that will please customers more. In many cases, better production processes actually lower costs and improve the customer experience – a true win/win. One simple, everyday example of innovation is the take-out window at fast-food restaurants. This is a simple innovation requiring no new technology or scientific breakthroughs. But it helped restaurants sell more in the same space and with only a small increase in the number of workers. At the same time, consumers appreciated the convenience of getting their food without stepping out of their car.

The concept of value added operates across the entire economy. A country's or region's GDP is the sum of all the value added in the economy. Individuals and companies that innovate and produce higher-value-added products and services will increase the GDP of a region – and usually earn higher wages and profits for themselves.

Rivalry Is the Third Element of Competitiveness

The world is not standing still. The rise and fall of Canada's fur trade between the sixteenth and nineteenth centuries demonstrate how traditional competitive strengths can erode as consumers' tastes change and remind us that we cannot stay passive amidst an ever-shifting global economy.

An industry closely tied to Canada's original founding and settlement, the fur trade took off in the late sixteenth century when wide-brimmed felt hats became popular in Europe, resulting in soaring demand for beaver pelts, from which the hats were made. Having exhausted European sources of felt, entrepreneurial fur traders crossed the Atlantic and flooded into the Canadian interior to tap into the region's abundant beaver supply and to trade European goods with the local Native population in exchange for pelts. Trade peaked in the eighteenth century, with annual pelt exports numbering in the hundreds of thousands. However, by the mid-nineteenth century, European tastes had begun to shift, and silk replaced felt in the manufacture of hats, causing beaver pelts to lose their value. As a result, the fur industry contracted in the latter half of the nineteenth century and never regained the prominent role it once held in Canada's economic history.

Through much of the twentieth century, Canadian pulp and paper producers enjoyed good growth, beginning with expansion outside Canada after the removal of the U.S. tariff on newsprint in 1913. Like other industries, pulp and paper suffered through the Great Depression. Growth resumed from the late 1940s though the 1960s. But since the 1970s, the industry has undergone ongoing challenges. The United States and Scandinavia became more capable competitors, and demand began to soften in some of our important markets around the world. During the 1980s, Brazil became a more potent player in pulp and paper.

One theme that seems constant as we look back over history is that building an economy around natural resources is fraught with risk. Whatever resource strength we may have currently, it's safe to say that rivals somewhere else in the world are exploring and developing strengths to match or surpass us. So, despite the insatiable appetite for resources, real prices have been coming down over the last two centuries as new sources are continually being found (Exhibit 3). While prices are currently buoyant, history tells us not to count on them staying high.

As with natural resources, our physical and human resources can be made less valuable by developments elsewhere. For example, North America's large auto-assembly facilities dominated the world until Japanese manufacturers found ways to reduce costs and improve quality, and American software developers broke out ahead of other countries with more engineering and computer power.

Most of us would rather do without rivalry from other people at work or other firms or other countries. But knowing that other people may get the job promotion if we don't improve our capabilities, or that another firm may be serving our customers better and putting our existence at risk, is a beneficial kind of pressure. It makes us better as individuals and firms. And it's an important factor in improving ourselves. That's what makes people and economies more prosperous.

Rivalry does not mean that one country's gain is another's loss. Rather, it means that the requirements for a nation's economic success are subject to change, because firms and people in other countries, and at home, are constantly looking to create their own advantage. This is beneficial for all of us – we are better off because of German precision

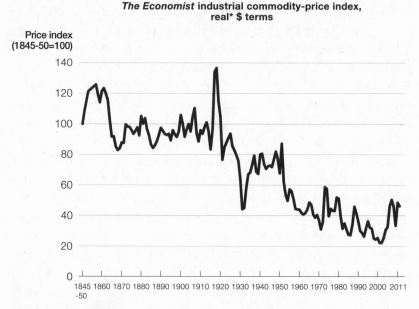

Exhibit 3 Commodity prices have been in long-term decline

The Economist **industrial commodity-price index,
real* $ terms**

Price index
(1845-50=100)

*Adjusted by U.S. GDP deflator.
Note: Based on twenty-five commodities including foods, industrial metals, non-food agricultural commodities (e.g., cotton, rubber, timber).
Sources: The Economist; Thomson Reuters.*

machinery or Chinese low-cost clothing. To be sure, development of new capabilities or advantages elsewhere can negatively affect some of our firms and industries. But our economy has to be sufficiently resilient and to provide adequate support for building our capabilities if we are to progress and not stand still.

Nobel Laureate Paul Krugman thinks it is a mistake to attribute 'competitiveness' to a country.[2] His main concern is that countries competing in the global economy should not be likened to competing firms. Typically, firms are contesting for a fixed amount of consumer spending on products or services. So, if the Schmidts buy a GM car today, that's lost revenue for Ford or Toyota. This is a zero-sum game. Apply this concept to countries, according to Krugman's line of reasoning, and the incorrect conclusion is reached that Japan's success in world markets comes at Canada's expense.

The next logical step is to focus on trade statistics. If Canada is running a trade surplus, exporting more than we're importing, then we're doing well. The balance of trade is like a firm's profit-and-loss statement. This can lead to some bad economic policy like adopting protectionism or focusing economic policy on export-oriented industries without recognizing that firms competing globally benefit from productive local, non-exporting firms.

But this is not how we understand a country's competitiveness. For us, competitiveness means drawing on a country's comparative advantages to create products and services of value to its own citizens and those around the world. We trade with other countries so that our consumers benefit from their comparative advantage. Our producers benefit greatly from using material or components made in other countries as they create their final products; similarly, many of our producers provide components to customers in other countries.

Throughout this book, we make international comparisons with Canada in areas like GDP or productivity. None of this is to suggest that we trail because we have lost some competitiveness battle with other countries. We compare Canada to other countries to measure how well we might be able to perform.

Harvard business strategist Michael Porter has no problem in ascribing the term competitiveness to countries' economic performance. He agrees entirely that the balance of trade is not the measure of competitiveness, and that economic progress is not a zero-sum game between countries. For him, a nation's increased competitiveness comes from improved productivity. Trade is important, but through its impact on productivity.[3]

Like Porter, we use the term competitiveness to describe a country's or a region's economic success. We don't use it in the sense that firms compete with each other.

Canada and Canadians cannot stand still. Like Michael Schmidt, they need to be constantly learning and upgrading their skills. Michael decided against following his father to a high-paying job on the assembly line. He's lucky, because the line closed while he was in university and his father had to take early retirement. And, while he was in the bank branch system, he saw that promotions there would be fewer and farther between as the branch network shrunk. By gaining technical skills, Michael was able to ride the wave to computerized banking. While at university and when he was struggling with his entry-level bank job, Michael was sometimes envious of his high school classmates who had taken good-paying jobs in manufacturing facilities. But his university education and ongoing skills enhancement have paid off in the long run. His kids always rolled their eyes when he stressed the need for lifelong learning – but they now know he was right.

Prosperity Is the Measure of Our Success

A nation's *prosperity* reflects the safe enjoyment of economic success by a wide range of its citizens and residents. Prosperity measures the income people are able to earn, and their access to the comforts of life, health care, and schooling, so that they can enjoy life today and invest in their future prosperity.

Prosperity also measures the happiness of a country's people. Academics often refer to this happiness as 'subjective well-being' – that is, whether people, in their own opinion, are happy with their life as it is. No doubt, there is more to prosperity than economic success. Several factors drive this broader measure of prosperity or happiness. Characteristics of life satisfaction include individual variables such as age, income, education, and mental health, as well as community variables like the size of the city region, percentage of the local population born in Canada and abroad, and the percentage of the local population with advanced education.[4]

The good news is that the vast majority of Canadians report high levels of satisfaction. Canada also scores near the top in global surveys of life satisfaction, such as the Gallup World Poll.

At first glance, people living in smaller, less populated settings are

Exhibit 4 **Income and other factors affect personal happiness**

Individual attribute	LOW life satisfaction associated with...	HIGH life satisfaction associated with...
Perceived mental health	Poor mental health	Excellent mental health
Perceived physical health	Poor physical health	Excellent physical health
Stress level	Extremely stressed	Not at all stressed
Sense of belonging to local community	Very weak sense of belonging	Very strong sense of belonging
Employment status	Disabled	Self-employed
Household income	**Lowest income decile**	**Highest income decile**
Marital status	Separated/divorced/ widowed	Married
Immigration status	Recent immigrants	Non-immigrants

Source: Centre for the Study of Living Standards, *Explaining Geographical Variation in Happiness in Canada*, November 2010, updated February 2011.

happier. On average, respondents in Ontario and British Columbia have slightly lower rates of happiness, while those in other provinces are more positive than the national average. People in larger cities like Toronto and Vancouver are less likely than the national average to be happy.

But most of these place-based differences disappear with deeper statistical analysis. Several factors consistently affected individuals' happiness (Exhibit 4).

Let's look at how Michael Schmidt's life is so much better than that of his parents and grandparents in so many ways:

• Life expectancy is higher. Michael's grandfather could expect to live fifty-nine years at his birth and his grandmother sixty-one years.

Life expectancy has increased for every generation. The Schmidt children had life expectancy of seventy-eight (Kevin) to eighty-three (Sandra and Louise) when they were born.

- Likelihood of attending college or university is higher. The percentage of population aged twenty to twenty-nine enrolled in post-secondary education has increased from 1 to 2 per cent before the Second World War to 17 per cent currently.
- More is spent per capita on health care. In 1937, the first year for which we have data, per-capita public expenditures on health care were $59 (2009 dollars). In 1960 they were $245; in 1989, $2,030; in 2009, $3,600.
- The time spent working has fallen from an average work week of more than forty hours in 1940 to thirty-five in 1980 and thirty-three in 2010, while real earnings have more than doubled.
- The time Michael needs to work to buy things like a new suit or a car is much lower as earnings have increased and costs decreased. His grandfather had to work seventy-four hours to afford a suit in 1940; this decreased to forty hours for his father in 1960 to only twenty-four hours for Michael himself. Similarly, his grandfather needed eight months of his wages to buy a car in 1940, while Michael needs only five months, and the car he buys is much safer, has air conditioning, and a state-of-the-art sound system.

Higher prosperity, then, affords improved well-being – typically through small changes in products, services, and costs that add up over time. These improvements remind us that we have made great economic progress over the years – even though currently we're not doing as well as we could. If we want to continue to raise our standard of living, we have to be relentless in our pursuit of higher competitiveness and prosperity.

Competitiveness and Prosperity Go Hand-in-Hand

Some argue that competitiveness and prosperity are two different things. Competitiveness is dark and sinister, they assert. It's about exploitation and gaining the upper hand. But shared prosperity is good.

It means good health and social outcomes, a clean environment, and broad-based trust.

We're the first to acknowledge that competitiveness and prosperity are different. But if competitiveness is the result of adding value to resources through a nation's advantages, and prosperity is about the safe enjoyment of the benefits of competitiveness, then it follows that a more competitive nation is very likely to be more prosperous. The two are not synonymous, but they are complementary.

It's hard to find a country or region that has built a competitive economy with a high GDP per capita where the benefits of that effort do not contribute to individuals' prosperity. For example, in Canada, personal income typically accounts for 80 per cent of GDP. That is, the lion's share of value added in the economy finds its way into people's income. Among the most prosperous economies, the ratio is similar to Canada's, at 75 per cent or higher.

Most of us are more prosperous than our forebears. Even those at the bottom of today's income ladder enjoy a higher standard of living than their counterparts in the past – through better access to the comforts of life and our social-safety net. And this higher prosperity comes from our ability to create economic value, our competitiveness.

One measure of the complementary nature of competitiveness and prosperity is our society's ability to afford public services and investments. As our GDP has risen, so too have public expenditures on various programs. For example, as noted earlier, public expenditure on health care has increased steadily over the years and now stands at $3,600 per capita. A similar trend can be seen in public expenditures on education. Those on the left may argue that governments are not spending enough and those on the right may say they're spending too much on health care and education. But it's clear that they would be spending less if our GDP performance had been lower over the last few decades. Programs like Medicare are possible only with robust economic competitiveness.

How Does Canada Fare?

Despite the current economic sluggishness here in Canada, we still

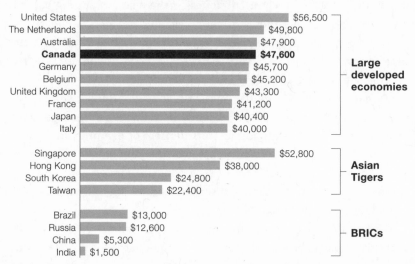

Exhibit 5 **Canada's GDP per capita leads most other countries**

2010 GDP per capita
(C$ 2010)

United States	$56,500
The Netherlands	$49,800
Australia	$47,900
Canada	**$47,600**
Germany	$45,700
Belgium	$45,200
United Kingdom	$43,300
France	$41,200
Japan	$40,400
Italy	$40,000

Large developed economies

Singapore	$52,800
Hong Kong	$38,000
South Korea	$24,800
Taiwan	$22,400

Asian Tigers

Brazil	$13,000
Russia	$12,600
China	$5,300
India	$1,500

BRICs

Source: Institute for Competitiveness & Prosperity analysis based on data from Statistics Canada; U.S. Bureau of Economic Analysis, U.S. Census Bureau; Australian Bureau of Statistics; Statistisches Bundesamt Deutschland; Centraal Bureau voor de Statistiek; INSEE – National Institute for Statistics and Economic Studies; Japan Statistics Bureau & Statistics Center; Statistics Singapore; Government of Hong Kong Special Administrative Region Census and Statistics Department; National Statistics Republic of China (Taiwan); Eurostat; IMF; World Bank; and OECD.

have one of the most vibrant economies in the world. We have a higher level of competitiveness and prosperity than most jurisdictions outside North America (Exhibit 5). Among these large economies, Canada has been in the top tier for the past decade. In 2010 it stood fourth among large economies. Among the Asian 'Tigers,' only the city state of Singapore surpasses Canada in GDP per capita.

We are also well ahead of the emerging BRIC countries – Brazil, Russia, India, and China. Despite all the current discussion on the success of these and other developing economies, they are a quantum behind Canada and other developed economies in competitiveness. The BRICs are not in the same economic league as we are. Their educational standards, their health care, their infrastructure, and their social cohesiveness fall well behind ours. By no means are we arguing for complacency – in

Exhibit 6 **GDP per capita is lower in Canada than the United States**

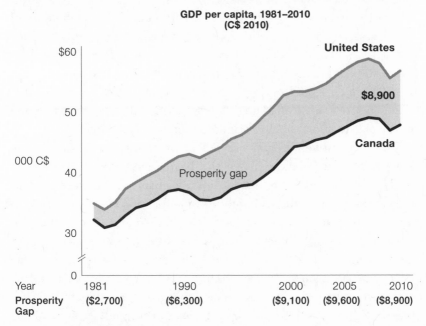

GDP per capita, 1981–2010
(C$ 2010)

Year	1981	1990	2000	2005	2010
Prosperity Gap	($2,700)	($6,300)	($9,100)	($9,600)	($8,900)

Note: Currency converted at PPP US$1 = C$1.203.
Source: Institute for Competitiveness & Prosperity analysis based on data from Statistics Canada and US Department of Commerce – Bureau of Economic Analysis.

fact, just the opposite. But we need to keep our relative competitiveness and prosperity in perspective.

Canadians should be proud that our economy is among the most competitive and prosperous in the world. We're not just nice – we're competitive. But compared to our neighbour and most significant trading partner, the United States, Canada's competitiveness has fallen behind and continues to lag. We conclude that we could be even more competitive and still be nice.

In the early 1980s, GDP per capita in Canada was $2,700 behind that of the United States. And since that time the gap has widened. In 2009, GDP per capita in Canada was $8,600 below that measure in the United States, and in 2010, the gap was virtually unchanged at $8,900 (Exhibit 6). This growing gap measures the degree to which the Canadian economy is not performing at full potential – even though performance is good by global standards.[5]

Our competitiveness gap is a prosperity gap, and it matters to all Canadians. Lagging competitiveness means lagging prosperity. Michael and Maria's parents wouldn't have experienced notable differences in living standards versus their U.S. counterparts. But Michael and Maria have seen their relative living standard drift farther and farther behind. If they're like many Canadians,[6] they're worried that their children will not be able to afford a better standard of living than they do.

The competitiveness gap has led to prosperity gaps for average Canadians, and for those above and below average. Because they're well established and have two incomes, Michael and Maria are around the eightieth percentile of family income in Canada – that is, one in five families enjoys higher income than they do, but four in five earn less. Back in the early 1980s, a family like the Schmidts enjoyed higher incomes than their U.S. counterparts. But over the years, as our GDP per capita has fallen farther behind that of the United States, the income of the Schmidts and other Canadians above the eightieth percentile has fallen behind their U.S. counterparts. Sandra Schmidt, being a single parent, is at the other end of the income spectrum – between the tenth and twentieth percentiles. Her income barely matches that of somebody at the same percentile in the United States, and the Canadian advantage at the lower end of incomes has narrowed as our GDP per-capita gap has widened.[7] Our prosperity gap has been felt more at upper-income levels, but even low-income Canadians run the risk of falling behind their U.S. counterparts.

In addition, government investment in Canada's future prosperity is constrained without a solid economic base. As we have seen, our economic growth generates public funds to afford excellent health care, education, and infrastructure. But we can't take economic growth for granted. Governments always have to make choices about where to cut and where to increase expenditures. These choices are tougher when they have less revenue.

Canadians have experienced these tough choices since the mid-1990s when governments had to cut spending to get our federal and provincial deficits under control. As spending was being forced to be more closely related to the revenues we actually had, our governments met their challenges by cutting back on both health-care and education spending. Health-care spending did return to its previous levels as our fiscal situation improved, but our education spending did not recover.

Canada cannot stand still. Emerging economies are at the stage of development where they compete on the basis of low-cost natural and human resources. Canada is endowed with many low-cost natural resources, but our prosperity comes from innovation and sophisticated human resources. Some or all of the developing economies will cross an 'innovation tipping point' when their product and process innovations, their design capability, and their consumers become more sophisticated. Rivalry will increase, and Canada needs to keep sharpening its competitiveness edge. But, we hasten to add, developing economies will not become more prosperous at Canada's expense. After the Second World War, we were forced to be more competitive, but Canadians didn't suffer as the German and Japanese people improved their competitiveness and standard of living.

Future success, however, is not guaranteed by current success. Even though economic development is not a zero-sum game globally, countries can and have fallen behind. The United Kingdom was ravaged by two world wars in the twentieth century and lost its global leadership. But more important, its stagnant economic performance – resulting from its own policy choices – hurt living standards for the average citizen.

Argentina is a more extreme example of how national fortunes can change.[8] At the close of the nineteenth century, Argentina's GDP per capita surpassed Canada's (it also surpassed that of the United States in 1897). It maintained rough parity with us through the start of the twentieth century until 1935. Under the leadership of Juan Peron, Argentina's economic policies included favouring domestic industries to replace imports, nationalizing key industries, and creating a single purchaser for the nation's export-oriented grain and oilseed industries, as well as wage freezes, subsidies, credit controls, and peso devaluations – often enforced by the military. Along the way, between 1932 and 1974, Argentina experienced 26 per cent annual inflation and fell farther and farther behind Canada and other developed countries. Today, Argentina's GDP per capita is less than one-fifth of Canada's.

Simply put, poor economic policies and poor performance have consequences for real people. And for Canada, there's our pride. We live in the best country in the world because of the wisdom and determination of our forebears – with some luck thrown in. Shouldn't we strive to have the best possible economic future we can? To help chart the course, it's important to understand where we have opportunities for achieving our prosperity potential. In the next chapter, we examine how much Canadians are working to achieve prosperity.

2 How Much Are We Working for Prosperity?

What is it that Canada is doing particularly well when we compare our performance to that of other countries around the world? And what is not going so well?

In a nutshell, Canada's economy grows because of our ability to create jobs. We have good demographics, a high percentage of our adults wanting to work, and a low unemployment rate by world standards. That's the good news. But when we're working, we're not adding as much value to the resources we work with as workers in most other economies. In the old cliché, versus their counterparts in other developed economies, Canadians work more but don't work smarter. Why? That's the issue we'll explore in this chapter.

At its simplest, we can say that economic output comes from two factors:

- how much work we are doing, expressed in hours per capita; and
- how much value we create when working, expressed as GDP per hour worked.

Our prosperity growth has been the result of both these factors – work effort and productivity (Exhibit 7).

Over the past two decades, the records of Canada and the United

Exhibit 7 **The source of prosperity is work effort and productivity**

Prosperity	Work effort			Productivity
	Profile	Utilization	Intensity	
GDP per capita =	$\dfrac{\text{Potential labour force}}{\text{Population}}$ X	$\dfrac{\text{Employed persons}}{\text{Potential labour force}}$ X	$\dfrac{\text{Hours worked}}{\text{Employed persons}}$ X	$\dfrac{\text{GDP}}{\text{Hours worked}}$

Source: Adapted from J. Baldwin, J.P. Maynard, and S. Wells, 'Productivity Growth in Canada and the United States,' *Isuma*, vol. 1, no. 1 (2000), Ottawa Policy Research Institute.

States with regard to these two factors have differed. Canada's significant divergence from the prosperity performance of the United States began during the recession of the early 1990s. During that time, the key factor driving our economic weakness was lower work effort, especially utilization and its two subelements, participation and employment. Since 1995, we have been successfully recovering to 1990 performance levels. But, at the same time, a growing productivity gap has emerged relative to the United States. Since the economic slowdown that began in 2008, unemployment has increased at a much faster rate in the United States than in Canada, while U.S. GDP performance has matched Canada's. With fewer workers contributing to the overall U.S. GDP, productivity per hour worked was higher than Canada's. The United States is achieving its current economic growth through productivity growth, not hours worked per capita. In Canada, our current growth is based on more of us working, not robust productivity improvement.

How much work we are doing is the result of three factors working together: profile, the percentage of our people who are able to work; utilization, how many of them are actually working; and intensity, how many hours in a day or a week or a year they are working. To dig down, we look at each of these three elements:

- *Profile.* Out of all the people in a jurisdiction, what percentage are of working age and therefore able to contribute to the creation of products and services that add economic value and prosperity?
- *Utilization.* For all those of working age, what percentage are actually working to add to economic value and prosperity? To gain further insight into this element, we examine the two contributors to utilization: *participation*, the percentage of those of working age who are searching for work, whether they are successful or not; and *employment*, the rate at which those participating in the job market are employed.
- *Intensity.* For all those who are employed, how many hours do they spend on the job in a year? This element measures both workers' desire to work more or fewer hours and the economy's ability to create demand for work hours.

These three factors – profile, utilization, and intensity – add up to our work effort, or the hours worked per capita. Together, they capture the human effort Canadians are expending to create economic value.

This chapter focuses on Canadians' work effort. The next chapter looks at how much value we are creating when we work, that is, our productivity. The question posed there is: For each hour worked in a jurisdiction, how much economic output is created by that jurisdiction's workers? Productivity measures how effectively our labour efforts add value to resources, thereby creating economic value and prosperity.

How Do the Three Elements Contribute to Our Overall Work Effort?

Profile Is an Advantage

Prosperity begins and ends with people. We need thinking and labouring workers to produce our prosperity; without them, we don't have prosperity – no matter how technologically advanced we become. To be sure, there are limits to the prosperity that we can create with labour effort. Nevertheless, workers are the foundation. Profile remains an advantage for Canada.

We define profile as the percentage of our population between the ages of fifteen and sixty-four – that is, the proportion of our population who can help create prosperity, not just consume it. Our children don't work, and so they are not part of our profile for prosperity. The same is true of our retired seniors. No doubt these limits are changing – many of our youth stay in school well past the age of fifteen; and many who are past the age of sixty-four continue to work. But, by and large, these are still useful borders for identifying the population who can work and contribute to our economic prosperity.

In Canada, between 65 and 70 per cent of our population are in this age bracket. This ratio has been stable over the short run and has had no appreciable impact on changes in our prosperity gap versus the United States (Exhibit 8). Compared to other advanced economies around the world, Canada has a marked profile advantage. In 2010, 69.4 per cent of Canadians were aged fifteen to sixty-four. Relative to the 67.0 per cent in the United States, Canada has a 3.5 per cent potential profile advantage.[1] Holding all other factors constant, we calculate this advantage to be worth $1,700 in per-capita GDP. In other words, because a higher proportion of our population is able to add to our prosperity, we have a profile advantage versus the United States. Compared to the United States, too, we have a slightly lower percentage of our population that is too young to work, but a higher proportion of working age. In both countries, the percentage of the population that is older than sixty-four is about the same.

Over the last few decades, Canada's demographic profile has stayed fairly constant. Immigrants have improved our demographic profile because they have tended to be younger on average than the Canadian host population – for example, compared to native-born Canadians, a higher percentage of immigrants in the 2006 Census were younger than forty-five and a lower percentage were forty-five or older. Our birth rates are keeping up with our retirement rates and, where our birth rate falls short, immigration partially fills the gap. Admittedly, as we are getting older, our profile will create less prosperity for our economy.

Exhibit 8 **Canada's demographics are a prosperity advantage**

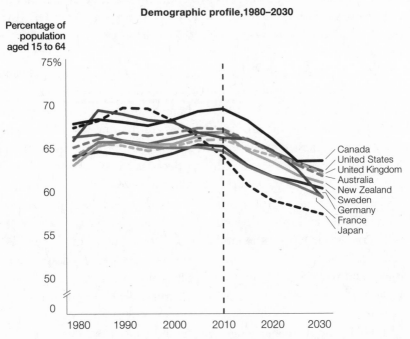

Demographic profile,1980–2030

Percentage of
population
aged 15 to 64

Source: Institute for Competitiveness & Prosperity analysis based on United Nations Population Statistics.

Nevertheless, Canada still has a solid demographic profile, and this is an excellent foundation on which to build our prosperity.

Our demographic challenges pale in comparison to those Europe faces, as birth rates there have declined steadily in the past few decades and immigration has not filled the gap. Germany and Italy have experienced especially low birth rates, with approximately eight and nine births per thousand population in the 2005–10 period. Canada and the United States, with eleven and fourteen births per thousand, fared reasonably well compared to these European nations. At the same time, net migration rates in most European nations have stagnated. In contrast, Canada outpaces other developed economies in this regard, while the United States is in the middle. For every 1,000 population, we have a net in-migration of 6.6 people; the United States has 3.3.

Europe's demographic challenges are not unique. Japan's birth rate stood at almost nine births per thousand, and the country is undergoing severe demographic problems with declining fertility and increasing dependency ratios. Moreover, Japan had a net migration rate of only 0.4.

Yet immigration, while important to Canada's population growth and human capital, will not be a major solution to its demographic challenges. The number of immigrants to Canada just simply isn't big enough to affect our demographic profile, regardless of their age profile.[2] Demographic projections indicate that the proportion of Canadians of working age will decline over the coming decades as baby boomers retire and are not replaced by equal numbers in subsequent generations. The projections indicate that Canada will maintain its advantage over the United States and other developed economies. Nevertheless, Canada will have fewer workers to create prosperity in the coming years. We estimate that by 2025 the smaller percentage of working-age Canadians will reduce GDP per capita potential by $3,100.[3] We will need creative retirement solutions to address this decline in our prosperity potential.[4]

Because of our greater longevity, the old rule of thumb about retiring at sixty-five no longer applies. It may be that seventy-five is the new sixty-five. Older workers have great skills and experience that our economy should be able to draw on, and they are more able and willing to keep working. One concern that has been raised in the context of an aging workforce is whether a shortage of skilled-trades workers is imminent. But our research shows that, while regional shortages may exist, we do not have a widespread skilled-trades shortage. (See sidebar on page 40.)

Utilization Means Creating Job Opportunities – and Canada Is a Leader

To what extent are we drawing on our endowed human capital? Utilization focuses on the proportion of our adults in the workforce.

Here, Canada is a world leader. Few, if any, countries are as success-ful in attracting adults to the workforce and in creating jobs for those who want them. Utilization, as we noted above, has two components – participation and employment.[5] *Participation* measures the percent-age of people aged fifteen or older who are willing and available to work. It includes those who are actually working and those who are searching for work. People who are not available for paid employ-ment – such as full-time students, family caregivers, and stay-at-home parents – are not part of the participation rate. Also excluded from the participation rate are people who are simply not looking for work – either because they perceive job prospects to be so scarce that job hunting is not worthwhile or for other reasons. This second group is the swing factor in labour markets. If the job market is robust, partici-pation rates will increase as discouraged workers re-enter the labour force.

In the 1980s and early 1990s, Canada led the United States in par-ticipation. But the recession that began in 1990 was very painful for Canada. Even though this recession officially ended in 1991, the par-ticipation rate continued to drift lower and did not reach bottom until 1996. As economic conditions improved, more adult Canadians rejoined the labour force, contributing to our economic potential. In 2010, 64.4 per cent of Canadians fifteen years of age and older worked or sought work.[6] The U.S. participation rate was 62.8 per cent. This advantage for Canada translates into $1,100 more in GDP per capita versus the United States. Canada also leads Australia, France, Germany, the Netherlands, and the United Kingdom. France is the participation-rate laggard – at 55 per cent in 2009.

In sum, our participation rates are above those in most other devel-oped economies. Canadians like working. And as we'll see, our econo-my excels at creating jobs for them.

One of the major participation trends in the past few decades has been the rising numbers of women entering the workforce. With birth rates declining and social attitudes changing, more women have decided to participate in the labour force – especially in Canada. In

Do we really have shortages in the skilled trades?

There seems to be daily press coverage on the lack of plumbers, pipefitters, plasterers, and other skilled trades. Governments have responded with programs to encourage apprenticeship and to help existing tradespeople. Young people are encouraged to get into the skilled trades.

We are skeptical of the risk of a long-term shortage of tradespeople. A real labour shortage will drive up wages, which in turn will attract more workers into the skilled trades. So, if there were shortages, we would expect to see wages growing faster among the trades than among all other occupations. However, while wages for the skilled trades are somewhat higher, they are not growing any faster (Exhibit A).

Let's examine supply and demand factors to help explain this counter-intuitive finding.

Regarding the *supply* of skilled-trades workers, the concern is that young people are not joining the trades to match the high percentage of tradespeople near retirement. But the average age for skilled-trades workers has been steady since 2004, while it has increased for all other occupations. Moreover, the number of older workers (55+) is about the same as younger workers (15–29).[a]

Apprenticeship registrations grew at an average annual rate of 9 per cent between 1996 and 2005, while skilled-trades employment growth averaged 2 per cent – indicating a low completion rate. What we have, then, is a retention issue, not evidence of a lack of interest by young people.

On the *demand* side, growth in skilled-trades employment has trailed growth across all other occupations. Unemployment rates typically don't differ; but in recessions, unemployment rates for those in skilled trades exceed those in all other occupations by about two to three percentage points.

These national statistics smooth over regional disparities. While trades growth in eastern Canada has been nil, it has been buoyant in the west – home of the resource industries. Unemployment among the skilled trades was particularly low in western Canada just prior to the 2008 recession. Strong economic growth in the west has strained the available supply of tradespeople, leading to temporary labour shortages there.

---

a   Wendy Pyper, 'Skilled Trades Employment,' Statistics Canada, *Perspectives*, Catalogue no. 75-001-X, October 2008.

Exhibit A **Wages among skilled trades and other occupations have grown at the same rate**

Hourly earnings, skilled trades versus all other occupations, 1997–2010 (C$ current)

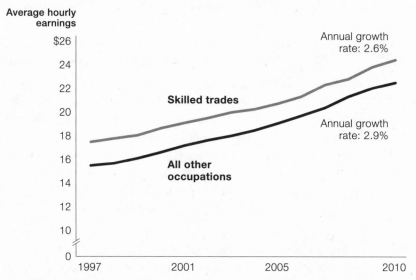

Note: Skilled trades are defined as NOC-S groups H1 (construction trades), H2 (electrical trades), H3 (machinists) and H4 (mechanics).
Source: Institute for Competitiveness & Prosperity analysis based on Statistics Canada, *Labour Force Survey.*

In manufacturing, some researchers conclude that skilled-trades shortages there are partially driven by the inability to attract workers at affordable wages.[b] The problem isn't labour shortages but unsustainable business models.

In summary, at a national level, there is little evidence to support the existence of a shortage of workers in the trades. However, there are challenges. Poor apprenticeship-completion rates, as well as legislative bottlenecks such as restrictive apprentice-journeyperson ratios, need to be addressed to avoid future skilled-trades shortages.

---

b Andrew Sharpe, Jean-Francois Arsenault, and Simon Lapointe, 'Apprenticeship Issues and Challenges Facing Canadian Manufacturing Industries,' Centre for the Study of Living Standards, February 2008.

the 1950s, 24.5 per cent of Canadian women worked or sought work, increasing to 31.3 per cent in the 1960s, 41.8 per cent in the 1970s, and 60.6 per cent in 2010. Strictly by the number of extra available workers since the 1970s (ignoring whether these workers had higher or lower skills than average), this phenomenon added $4,500 GDP per capita in Canada.

Maria Schmidt's family typifies this trend. Her mother worked off and on to make ends meet, and her mother-in-law was a traditional stay-at home mom. Maria and two of her sisters are now full-fledged 'participants' in the labour market. Maria's daughter Sandra is in the labour force and Louise expects to be once she's finished her schooling. This story repeats itself in many Canadian families.

The other component of utilization is *employment*. This measures labour-force participants' success in finding jobs. Economic analysts and politicians await the monthly results with great interest. Statistics Canada and counterparts around the world report the unemployment rate in the previous month. The unemployment rate measures the percentage of people who are available to work but are not working. Economists tell us that the lowest this rate can realistically fall to is around 4 per cent – what they call the 'full employment' rate. Zero unemployment is not achievable. Even in the most booming economy, there will be layoffs here and there. Some people will have quit their job to find something better and be between jobs. Newly graduated students will be entering the labour force and have not yet found the right job. There's also geographic friction. As fisheries close in the Atlantic, jobs go unfilled in Alberta's oil sands since workers can't just pick up and move. Eventually, however, many workers do just that – or at least find ways to travel the long distances from work to home, as we see with eastern Canadians commuting to western resource jobs.

Unemployment rates have gotten as high as 20 per cent – that's what Canada and the United States experienced in the Great Depression. In the past five recessions in Canada, unemployment rates reached a

Exhibit 9 **Canada has higher participation and lower unemployment rates than the United States**

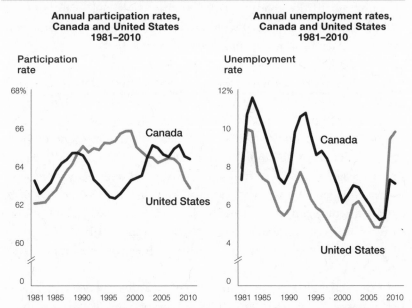

Annual participation rates,
Canada and United States
1981–2010

Annual unemployment rates,
Canada and United States
1981–2010

Note: Participation rates calculated as labour force divided by population 15+. Canada unemployment rates are consistent with U.S. methodology.
Source: Institute for Competitiveness & Prosperity analysis based on data from Statistics Canada; U.S. Census Bureau, U.S. Bureau of Labor Statistics, Current Population Survey.

maximum monthly rate that ranged between 8 and 13 per cent. In the Unites States, recessionary unemployment ranged between 6 and 11 per cent.

Canada has traditionally had higher unemployment rates than the United States, but not much higher. Since 2000, our average annual unemployment rate was 6.3 per cent versus 6.0 per cent in the United States (Exhibit 9). Unemployment rates increased in both countries in the recession beginning in 2008, but the problem was more severe in the United States. In 2010 the United States suffered from higher unemployment, 9.8 per cent, than Canada, where the unemployment rate stood at 7.1 per cent, down from 7.3 per cent[7] in 2009. This 2.7 percentage-point advantage lifted our relative GDP per-capita performance by $1,400 in 2010.

Compared to other advanced economies outside North America, Canada has enviably low unemployment rates. But it's worth pointing to two factors about the unemployment rate that public discussion should take into account.

First, the base for the unemployment rate is the people actually looking for work, those who make up the participation rate. As recessions drag on, unemployment rates can start to fall as people simply drop out of the labour market – hence the denominator in the unemployment calculation falls and the unemployment rate also falls. Sometimes, we get a 'false positive' signal from good unemployment news. In just the opposite way, as the economy begins to come out of its slump, discouraged workers get back into the job market, and this can increase reported unemployment. It pays to look at both the unemployment and the participation rates to see how the economy is really performing.

Second, changes in the unemployment rate are only one factor in the performance of our economy. It sounds impressive if the unemployment rate drops a full point from 6 per cent to 5 per cent. But it also means that employment has increased from 94 per cent to 95 per cent, which in the scheme of things does not drive a major increase in our economic output.

Neither Maria nor Michael has been officially unemployed for long periods. Michael joined the bank right out of school, and so he would always have shown up as employed in Statistics Canada's monthly Labour Force Survey. And he has stayed with the bank through his working career. Maria has not worked for pay constantly, but for the times she didn't work she was not looking for a job – and so was not participating in the labour force.

When we bring together participation rates and unemployment rates, we have the percentage of our working-age population who are actually working – or the rate at which we are utilizing our potential workforce. Currently, Canada has a utilization advantage over the

United States and most other advanced economies. Traditionally, we have trailed the United States in this measure, but the 2008 downturn dramatically affected U.S. performance and Canada now leads. In 2010, Canada employed 59.8 per cent of its working-age population, above the U.S. result of 56.7 per cent. This superior performance translates into a $2,500 utilization advantage in GDP per capita – the combined effect of a $1,100 participation advantage and a $1,400 employment advantage.

Intensity Captures Time on the Job – and Canadians Work More Hours Than Most Others, but Fewer Than Our U.S. Counterparts

To this point, we have treated all jobs as the same, without differentiating between the hours worked per job. Clearly, a worker at a part-time job does not create as much economic value as one at the same job on a full-time basis. Nor does a worker on vacation for half the month create as much value as someone on the same job for the full month. These factors affect our economic output.

It is almost a truism that, as societies become more economically successful, the average worker spends fewer hours on the job (Exhibit 10). As earnings increase, people become satiated with the goods and services they have been able to purchase, and they become more interested in having leisure time – the extra day tacked on to their long weekend or the restful vacation at their cottage. At some point, they value their unpaid leisure time more than the extra dollars they earn by spending more time on the job.

The subject of intensity – hours worked per employed person – has recently attracted attention from economists and those involved with public policy. For some, the key challenge is to ensure that, as our society prospers, the number of hours that workers are on the job declines. This has appealing logic. Leisure is an important contributor to health and well-being. Overworked individuals are less happy and less effective on the job. And some workers may not have adequate employment opportunities because others are working too many

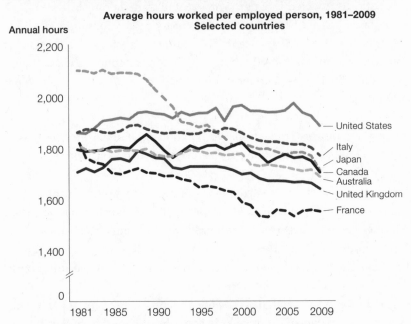

Exhibit 10 **Workers in Canada and most other developed economies spend fewer hours on the job than U.S. counterparts**

Average hours worked per employed person, 1981–2009
Selected countries

Annual hours

Source: Institute for Competitiveness & Prosperity analysis based on data from Statistics Canada; U.S. Census Bureau, U.S. Bureau of Labor Statistics, *Current Population Survey*; and OECD.

hours, contributing to significant underemployment, especially among less-educated individuals.

Others note that there is a downside to working less. In Canada, the intensity gap with the United States has grown significantly over the past thirty years. We now work about three hours per week less than our neighbours to the south. The gap has grown because Canadians are taking more weeks away from work, and because we are working fewer hours in the weeks when we are at work. At the same time, U.S. workers were working about the same number of hours annually – although average hours worked per worker have declined in the United States in the current downturn.

This gap cumulates to an annual difference of 167 hours, or nearly four and a half weeks, that each worker spends on the job annually. We estimate that, for 2010, the intensity gap accounted for $4,700 of the $8,900 per-capita prosperity gap. Closing some of this intensity gap has the potential to contribute to higher prosperity for individuals and families. We could also generate significant additional government revenue. This would make possible both higher investment in education and health care and lower taxes.

We agree, however, with the general proposition that closing the prosperity gap primarily through increased work effort is an unwise course. It goes against the idea of working smarter, not harder, to increase prosperity. It is also impractical if it works against individual preferences. But we do not conclude that public policy should be geared toward reducing work hours to match the situation in Europe, where regulations limit work hours more than in North America, since there is no evidence that this practice can or should be transplanted.

Whether we need new approaches to deciding the right amount of time workers spend on the job ought to be informed by a deeper understanding of the labour market in Canada. While there are many similarities in workforces in Canada and the United States and the time they spend on the job, two differences stand out clearly: vacations are longer in Canada and there is also a greater incidence here of part-time work. As a result of both factors, Canadians are away from their jobs more than their U.S. counterparts (Exhibit 11).

The most important reason why more Canadian than U.S. workers are employed part-time is that they are unable to find full-time work – this accounts for 30 per cent of the difference in part-time employment between the two countries. Economic conditions are the major determinant. In the past few decades, when unemployment was higher, involuntary part-time employment increased. In a sense, we have a vicious circle – lower productivity leads to worse economic conditions that, in turn, reduce the demand for labour, especially among the less skilled. This lower work effort reduces our prosperity, and so on. Among the other reasons we have advanced for investing in education, this points to the ongoing imperative to raise Canadians' skills,

Exhibit 11 **Vacations and a greater incidence of part-time work are the key differences in hours worked between Canada and the United States**

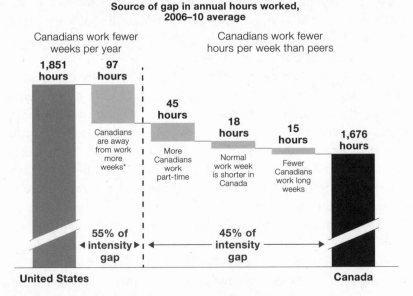

Source of gap in annual hours worked,
2006–10 average

* Mostly vacations.
Source: Institute for Competitiveness & Prosperity based on Statistics Canada, *Labour Force Survey*;
U.S. Census Bureau, U.S. Bureau of Labor Statistics, *Current Population Survey*.

since involuntary part-time work is more prevalent among those with lower skills. We need to continue working to ensure that our children are staying in school, so that they are less vulnerable to the vicissitudes of economic downturns and the employment market.

The intensity gap is wider among our more productive workers. Compared to their U.S. counterparts, Canadian workers with higher education and higher incomes take more weeks off work (Exhibit 12) and are less likely to work long work weeks, defined as fifty or more hours per week. While there are no significant differences in our overall propensity to work more hours for greater prosperity, the most highly educated and the highest income earners are less interested than their U.S. peers in working longer hours to augment their prosperity.[8] Also,

Exhibit 12 **As income increases in Canada, the vacation gap with U.S. counterparts widens**

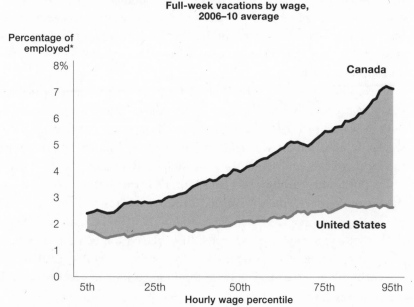

Full-week vacations by wage,
2006–10 average

* Taking a vacation one week or longer in any given month.
Source: Institute for Competitiveness & Prosperity based on Statistics Canada, *Labour Force Survey*;
U.S. Census Bureau, U.S. Bureau of Labor Statistics, *Current Population Survey*.

while there is a solid wage premium paid to people with higher educational attainment, this premium is higher in the United States. As we'll see, the premium paid for creativity-oriented workers, who typically are more highly educated, is higher in the United States.

This is part of what we refer to as the 'tuning' of the Canadian economy. Our economy does not value higher-skilled workers and managers as much as the U.S. economy does. This is one of the reasons we have fewer workers with university degrees. It also helps explain why Canadians at the highest income levels work fewer hours than their U.S. counterparts – the incentive for Canadians to work longer hours is lower. What we think is happening in the United States is that people with the highest skills have the opportunity to earn much higher incomes by investing in more work hours (immediately or in the long term as their careers develop) and so they choose less vacation time. In Canada, the earnings 'pop' for our most highly skilled workers is not as pronounced – hence, their choice of more leisure. Consequently, our overall productivity is lower. Each of our two economies operates consistently. The U.S. economy is tuned to a higher level of innovation and sophistication.

Maria and Michael are typical. At the start of his career, Michael put in many long hours to get his career going. He often was too busy with the latest project or client to take all three of his entitled vacation weeks. In addition, he was teaching a course on financial planning at the local college, and the extra work helped the young family financially. But, as his earnings rose and Maria's earnings began to add up, the Schmidts decided they wanted to smell the roses. They invested in a cottage and really valued their downtime together and with their kids. As they got more prosperous, they placed a much higher value on the extra week of vacation than on the extra money they could earn by working more. Michael stopped teaching and made sure he took all his vacation days.

To the extent that Canadians, like the Schmidts, are content to work less and to enjoy the benefits of their prosperity, that is an attractive feature for many families. But, to the extent that those who want to work more to advance their economic situation are being constrained, we need to create opportunities for them to work and earn more. And, to the extent that we are underutilizing the potential contribution from our more productive workers, we need to look for creative solutions to help them make a greater contribution to higher prosperity.

Taken together, the three work-effort factors – profile, utilization, and intensity – account for just $500 of the Canada-U.S. prosperity gap of $8,900. The balance of the gap – $8,400 – is the result of lagging productivity, which we'll discuss in the next chapter.

In conclusion, Canada is not missing its prosperity potential because we're not working. We have a solid demographic base so that more of us are of working age. We're more attached to the workforce than most others. Our economy is very successful at creating jobs. It's true that we spend fewer hours on the job compared with our U.S. counterparts, but we work more than people in most other countries. Our challenge isn't our low work effort – it's our lack of effectiveness when we're working.

3 How Much Value Are We Creating When We Are Working?

Canadians put more work effort into our prosperity than our counterparts around the developed world (Exhibit 13). This is partly due to structural factors – our demographics mean that more of us are of working age. But most of the advantage is because of our choices and policies. So, if more of us are working than nearly everybody else, why do we have a prosperity gap? It's because when we're working, we're not as productive as our counterparts in other developed economies. (See sidebar on page 54.)

Lagging productivity is our biggest challenge. As a concept, productivity is often misunderstood. Earlier we explained that GDP is the sum of all the value added by our workers and firms across the economy. At its very simplest, we can make GDP grow by working more – through a better demographic mix, with more adults choosing to work and successfully finding jobs, and by working more hours on the job – or by creating more value in the hours we work. The latter option requires elaboration. It's easy to visualize Maria returning to the workforce or Michael putting in extra hours, which are part of work effort. But how do they create value in a work hour? As we'll see, workers' ability to create more value per hour worked can come from many different sources, such as more education and training, clustering of people and

Exhibit 13 **Canada is near the top in work effort but trails productivity leaders significantly**

Work effort, productivity, and prosperity, 2009 (C$2010)

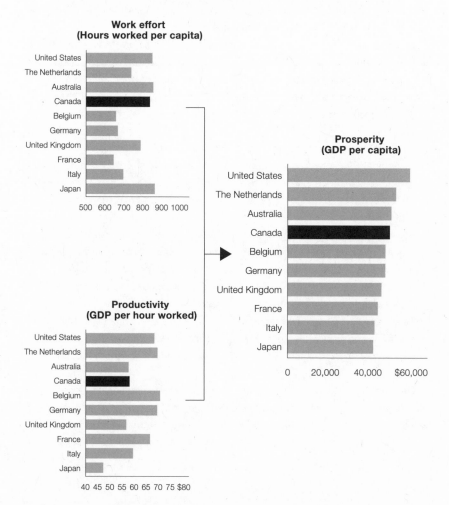

Note: Data are from the year 2009 and converted to 2010 dollars at PPP = 1.203.
Source: Institute for Competitiveness & Prosperity analysis based on data from Statistics Canada; U.S. Bureau of Economic Analysis, U.S. Census Bureau, U.S. Bureau of Labor Statistics, *Current Population Survey*; Australian Bureau of Statistics; Statistisches Bundesamt Deutschland; Centraal Bureau voor de Statistiek; INSEE – National Institute for Statistics and Economic Studies; Japan Statistics Bureau & Statistics Center; Eurostat; IMF; and OECD.

Canadians work more but not smarter

We identify Canada's international 'peers' as those countries with at least ten million people and with the highest GDP per capita.[a]

Only the *United States* gains its prosperity through above-average work effort and productivity (see Exhibit 13). Most European countries rank high in productivity but not work effort. Lower-skilled workers are less engaged in the economy; higher-skilled workers drive productivity. By contrast, Australia, Canada, the United Kingdom, and Japan have wider labour-force participation but achieve lower productivity.

The Netherlands performs well in GDP per capita, but its labour-force characteristics differ significantly from Canada's. Its participation rate is much higher than that of others on the Continent. However, hours worked per employed individual are much fewer. Its high productivity puts the Netherlands ahead of Canada in GDP per capita.

Australia's geography is similar to Canada's, with urban centres separated by sparsely populated rural regions and a significant resource base. Australia exports a large amount of processed and unprocessed natural resources – but to Asia, not the United States. Australia's GDP per capita slightly leads Canada's, with very similar work effort and productivity performance.

Belgium ranks between its French and Dutch neighbours in prosperity. Its lower labour-force engagement is more like France's than the Netherlands', but its workers work more hours. Belgium led all of the peers with the highest productivity level in 2009.

Germany trails Canada in prosperity. The legacy of reunification continues. While some of its states are very competitive by international standards, the country as a whole does not lead. Like others in continental Europe, Germany has a significantly lower labour-force participation rate than Canada, and its workers work fewer

---

a   The population criterion excludes smaller but prosperous countries like Sweden and Switzerland. While their specific policies are of interest, these countries do not have the size and breadth of economic challenges to make them comparable to Canada. The prosperity criterion eliminates countries like Korea, Egypt, and the BRIC countries. China, for example, is important, given its growth and trade performance. However, its current GDP per capita is $5,300, only one-ninth of Canada's.

hours. Its productivity advantage versus Canada does not compensate for its lower work effort; hence it trails in GDP per capita.

While GDP per capita is lower in the *United Kingdom* than in other English-speaking countries, it looks much more like them than continental Europe. Its work effort is slightly less than Canada's and so is its productivity.

France symbolizes the Continent, with much lower labour-force engagement than Canada – even lower than Germany. Those who are employed tend to work a moderate number of hours – more than in Germany or the Netherlands but much fewer than in countries beyond the Continent. France achieves a high level of productivity, since many lower-skilled individuals are not in the workforce. The lower work effort overwhelms France's productivity advantage, and so its prosperity trails Canada's considerably.

With its two distinct economies, *Italy* is like Germany. The economic engine in Italy's north is comparable to the best in France and Germany, with high GDP per capita. However, when averaged out with Italy's southern economy, Italy's prosperity trails Canada's markedly. Compared to Canada, Italy has slightly higher productivity but much lower work effort.

Japan differs from our European peers, with relatively high participation rates and a high number of hours worked per employed person. However, Japan's traditional work-effort advantage has been eroding. Its productivity also trails, and so does GDP per capita.

---

businesses to enhance economic activity, greater investment in technology, and more innovative business strategies by employers.

Let's go back to our sandwich example. How can waiters or cooks at the sandwich shop improve their productivity? How can they add more value per hour?

If the shop owner can develop an interesting new and complementary concept – say, Italian Panini and meatball specialties – the restaurant can attract more customers, thereby generating more revenue with the existing staff of waiters and cooks. Then value added per hour will increase in several ways. Food spoilage will likely be lower, because turnover increases; wages may rise as people work more hours, but probably not as much as the business improves;

heat, light, and power costs will go up only a little to handle the extra traffic.

Not all the extra revenue from the accompanying higher sales finds its way to value added. To make the extra sales, the restaurant has to buy more bread and other food, and these costs have to be subtracted from the revenue. And extra energy will be required to heat the stoves for any additional cooking time. In this scenario, the workers have done little to raise productivity, because they have not added much extra value each hour they worked.

But, if the shop owner finds that he can increase prices for sandwiches by making the restaurant more visually appealing or by having evocative names for his sandwiches without losing customers, productivity actually goes up. Much of the higher price then raises the restaurant's profits. Value added has increased.

Alternatively, the restaurant owner may decide to streamline operations significantly. Through better design of the space and improved use of technology to speed up the time in which an order is taken and communicated to the kitchen, perhaps through the addition of a drive-through window, the restaurant owner may be able to attract more customers. Throw in a price reduction, and the volume goes up even more. After accounting for all the increased capital costs and the additional staff, the owner hopes to find that he's created more revenue than costs. Value added per hour worked has increased, even though his wage bill is higher because there are more people working.

Some observers think that productivity improvements are good for owners and capitalists but not for workers – that they mean more for the bottom line than for the workers. It is, of course, possible for all the benefits of the productivity improvements to accrue to the restaurant owner. But workers do share in the benefits of productivity improvements. At the very least, as business improves, more workers will likely be needed, and the restaurant will be paying more wages. And often, as innovation occurs, the restaurant's managers and waiters will require more skills to be more adept with technology or customer relations.

These requirements for advanced skills typically mean higher wages. Either the restaurant will invest in training its current workers to secure these skills, or it will gradually turn over its workforce, hiring new workers with the required skills.

To be sure, as the restaurant's innovation and productivity improve, less skilled waiters and managers may be let go. We are certainly experiencing this phenomenon across our economy. As our firms and economy become more sophisticated, workers with the requisite skills do well. Those without the right skills run a great risk of being left behind in dead-end jobs or being unemployed.

Another criticism of these productivity-enhancing scenarios may be that they are still all a zero-sum game. Our restaurateur may have gained customers, but only at the expense of other restaurants or of other places where people used to spend their money. This is an intuitively attractive argument, but it's wrong. As people shift their spending to restaurants that better meet their needs, their satisfaction (or what economist call 'utility') increases. And restaurants that were offering less value will lose customers – or in some cases go out of business. Waiters leaving the faltering restaurants can be hired at the growing restaurants. Through the development of higher-value-added products and services and the shifting of labour and capital resources to them, productivity across the economy has increased.

In another example, free trade between Canada and the United States opened opportunities for capable manufacturers to grow through expanded access to the U.S. market and severely threatened less capable manufacturers. Some responded to the challenge and improved their operations, but others simply went out of business. In effect, capital and labour resources shifted from weak operators to strong operators, who delivered more products and services. This shift increased our overall productivity.[1]

While not necessarily true in the case of our thriving restaurant, consumers' dollars can go further when the suppliers of goods and services to them are more productive. Staying in the food-service business, McCain added to our country's productivity by finding a way to deliver frozen French fries to restaurants. This meant that the restaurant owner did not have to devote resources to peeling and cutting potatoes and saved money by buying the frozen fries from McCain. These savings could be reinvested in the business, used to cut prices, or taken out as higher profits by the owner. At the same time, McCain's employed many workers in its manufacturing facility in New Brunswick and invested in new capital equipment. As if through alchemy, new economic activity and prosperity were created.

There are two important lessons in the McCain story. First, productivity and innovation in our economy are achieved through myriad incremental improvements. Replacing potatoes peeled and cut in the restaurant with frozen fries from a central source was a small improvement in restaurants' operations and productivity. Multiply that many times in a year and across the economy and you get an ongoing march toward better productivity growth and an improvement in our economic well-being. Second, the source of this productivity gain was an idea – a product of human ingenuity. Creating the environment for such ideas to be generated and brought to reality is the key to improving our productivity and innovation.

Productivity Has No Limits

One way to improve living standards is to work more hours or use up more and more of our natural and physical resources. But this is constraining. We can find new workers from our population up to a point. But there are only so many hours in a day and days in a year. Natural resources are limited or become too costly to acquire and, in addition, their use can have adverse environmental consequences.

The other way is to improve productivity. And the only limit to productivity growth is human ingenuity and innovation. Productivity measures how much value we create per unit of resources used – whether the resources are an hour of labour, an hour of machine time, a barrel of oil, or any other scarce resource. The value created is

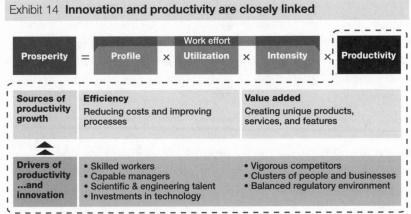

Exhibit 14 **Innovation and productivity are closely linked**

Source: Institute for Competitiveness & Prosperity.

represented by how much money somebody will pay for the output – above and beyond the value of resources used. Productivity increases in one of two ways – greater efficiency in the use of inputs or higher value added per unit of input (Exhibit 14):

- Efficiency gains come about from any number of different process innovations: better organization of work, automation, improved economies of scale, and so on.
- Higher value added comes from adding innovative unique product or service features for which consumers will pay more than the added cost to the producer.

Unfortunately, many people understand productivity improvements to come only from higher efficiency and this in turn is often associated with layoffs or outsourcing of work. But that is only one part of the productivity story. Equally, if not more, important is the productivity growth from new value creation. Individuals and businesses that add more value to resources through unique skills, products, and services are more productive.

Productivity is value added dollars per hour worked. Efficiency, expressed as units of output per hour, can be an element of productivity, but it's not necessarily the case. British researchers[2] studied productivity differences in the biscuit manufacturing industry in Britain and Germany between 1989 and 1992. Using a single measure, tons produced per employee, they found that British manufacturers were 20 per cent more 'productive' than their German counterparts. But the researchers then adjusted for differing quality between the two countries. They found that the average biscuit produced in Germany was much more elaborate than the average one produced in Britain. When they calculated sales revenue less the cost of ingredients (value added), they found that productivity was 45 per cent higher in the German industry.

Many of us remember the first entry of Japanese auto manufacturers to North America in the 1980s. They were making great strides in straight efficiency, vehicles produced per worker hour, and that is indeed productivity. But at the same time their quality was superior to cars produced by North American manufacturers. Domestic producers had to discount their cars significantly to move them off the lots, while Japanese cars typically sold for full value. That, too, is productivity.

At the business level, which is the source of much a jurisdiction's productivity, strategies that successfully lead to products and services for which people will pay a premium will drive regional productivity higher. An efficient producer turning out products and services that require price incentives to stimulate consumer demand is not as productive as a facility producing cars that are in great demand at premium prices. The challenge for Canada – and for all jurisdictions – is to create the environment in which management teams are developing breakthrough value-added products and services.

Jurisdictions that attract and foster these individuals and businesses are more productive. For example, Ontario's wine industry has become more productive as it has moved to higher-quality wines and introduced ice wine to the world, since producers can now charge more for products that consumers value more highly.

Rising Productivity Has Driven Our Past Economic Growth

At one time, today's developed economies were mostly agrarian, and farmers manually worked the land and spread the seeds. Investment in machinery, such as tractors and threshers, and innovations, such as high-yield seeds and new crop-rotation methods, dramatically reduced the amount of work and workers needed to produce the same output of agricultural products.[3] Farmers out of work headed toward the urban centres, where many found jobs in newly emerging manufacturing plants producing all sorts of consumer goods.

Eventually, technological and process innovations occurred in all areas of manufacturing, and output increased faster than employment. Productivity gains were clear in the vast increases of output with the same amount of labour. Workers then moved on from their assembly-line jobs to retail stores, food services, medicine, engineering, management, and other professional industries.

Productivity gains have propelled advanced economies in the past decades. Canada and all the advanced economies we consider our peers have improved their competitiveness and prosperity through higher productivity. Increased work effort has been important, but much less so (Exhibit 15).

The greatest spikes in productivity have historically been associated with specific technological innovations. The steam engine, electricity, and assembly lines are among the most important technological innovations that have led to higher productivity growth. More recently, computers and the Internet have been associated with more productivity.

Since most of the value created in an economy goes to workers in the form of wages, productivity growth means higher wages; the relationship between productivity and wages across Canada and the United States is very strong (Exhibit 16). Productivity also means that more innovative and lower-cost products and services are available for everyday use.

Exhibit 15 **Economies grow most through higher productivity**

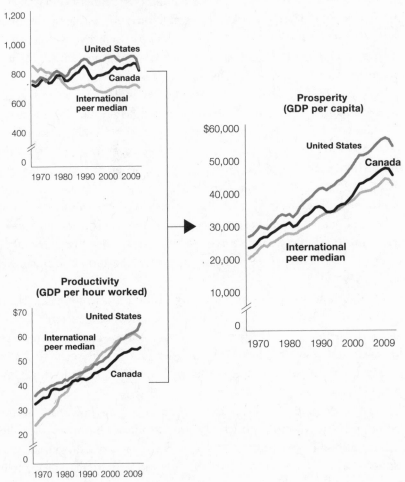

Work effort, productivity, and GDP per capita, 1970–2009
Canada and international peers (C$2009)

Work effort
(Hours worked per capita)

United States

Canada

International
peer median

1970 1980 1990 2000 2009

Prosperity
(GDP per capita)

United States

Canada

International
peer median

1970   1980   1990   2000   2009

Productivity
(GDP per hour worked)

United States

International
peer median

Canada

1970 1980 1990 2000 2009

Note: Currency converted at 2009 PPP US$1=C$1.178.
8 peer countries: Australia, Belgium, France, Germany, Italy, Japan, Netherlands, United Kingdom.
Source: Institute for Competitiveness & Prosperity analysis based on data from Statistics Canada;
U.S. Bureau of Economic Analysis, U.S. Census Bureau, U.S. Bureau of Labor Statistics; OECD.

Exhibit 16 **Across North America, productivity and wages are tightly linked**

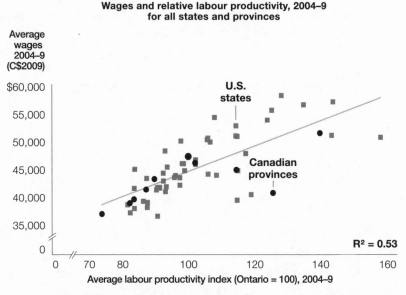

Wages and relative labour productivity, 2004–9
for all states and provinces

*Productivity is defined as GDP/hours worked.
Source: Institute for Competitiveness & Prosperity analysis based on data from Statistics Canada; U.S. Bureau of Economic Analysis (GDP); U.S. Bureau of Labor Statistics, Occupational Employment Statistics (Wages); CPS microdata (U.S. hours worked).

Productivity Drives a Jurisdiction's Competitiveness and Standard of Living

Competitiveness expert Michael Porter stresses the importance of productivity:

> To understand competitiveness, the starting point must be the underlying sources of prosperity. A nation's standard of living is determined by the productivity of its economy, which is measured by the value of goods and services produced per unit of the nation's human, capital, and natural resources. Productivity depends both on the value of a nation's products

and services, measured by the prices they can command in open markets, and the efficiency with which they can be produced.

True competitiveness, then, is measured by productivity. Productivity allows a nation to support high wages, a strong currency, and attractive returns to capital – and with them a high standard of living. Productivity is the goal.[4]

Canada is currently on a troublesome trend of falling farther and farther behind its peers in productivity growth. Reports by the Organisation for Economic Co-operation and Development (OECD) on productivity growth among its member nations repeatedly show how Canada's performance lags. Productivity accounts for the greatest share of our prosperity gap. This lost potential reduces opportunities for us all, since higher productivity is the key to raising living standards for all Canadians.

Canada also trails in various innovation measures. Compared to other OECD countries, we are laggards in using technology in our businesses. Despite large investments by government in R&D, our businesses' rate of R&D investment falls behind that of many other OECD countries. And we also trail when it comes to registering patents.

Canada has one of the most globally competitive economies. The main challenge is to improve its productivity to achieve its full prosperity potential for the benefit of all Canadians. Higher productivity is critical to our success. And improving our productivity means improving our innovation performance.

PART TWO

What Drives Our Productivity and Innovation Performance?

So far, we've concluded that productivity and innovation are very close-ly related – and are highly important contributors to a nation's pros-perity. It's here where Canada trails. So what are the challenges we face in improving our productivity? In chapters 4 through 6, we turn to the three drivers of productivity and innovation performance (Exhibit 17):

First, where we live and work (chapter 4):

- Urban regions are the centres of innovation and creativity – and to the extent our people live and work in these settings, we will be more productive.
- Clusters of people and businesses stimulate cooperation, competi-tion, and new ideas in industries that innovate.

Second, how we compete (chapter 5):

- Firms and industries that compete on the basis of innovation and creativity will be more productive and so will the nations in which they operate.
- Innovation is the result of a good balance between pressure and support.

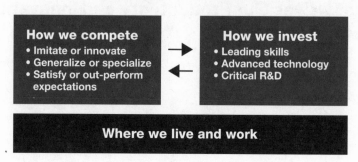

Exhibit 17 **How we compete and how we invest drive our economic performance**

Drivers of economic performance

How we compete
• Imitate or innovate
• Generalize or specialize
• Satisfy or out-perform expectations

How we invest
• Leading skills
• Advanced technology
• Critical R&D

Where we live and work

And third, how we invest (chapter 6):

• Workers and managers who have gained skills through education and training adapt more quickly to changing circumstances – on the job and over time; and contribute ideas for product, service, and process improvements.
• Investments in technology aimed at automating the routine elements of work support better products and services and enable entirely new business models which make workers and businesses more productive and innovative.

Where we live and work is really a baseline for economic success. It is very difficult to achieve a large-scale shift of people from rural to urban settings. And try as they might, governments have had little success in changing the industrial makeup of a state or province. In some sense, where we live and where we work is the hand we've been dealt.

Within this environment, the key factors are how we compete and how we invest so our economy performs better. How we compete is defined by whether our businesses strive to be world leaders in innovating products and services or merely adapt breakthroughs made elsewhere to the domestic market. Do our businesses survive simply by satisfying current consumer demand or are they constantly pressured to achieve superior performance? How we compete informs how we invest. An economy operating on imitation instead of innovation does not really need ongoing investment in technology or R&D. Nor do its workers require skills that are unsurpassed in the world.

These latter two factors – how we compete and how we invest – are typically 'in tune' with each other – or in equilibrium, as economists would say. We conclude that Canada is perfectly in tune – how we invest drives how we compete and vice versa in a virtuous/vicious circle. But we're tuned to a lower level of sophistication than other countries with higher productivity. We need to raise our aspirations and take the necessary actions to achieve our full prosperity potential.

4 How Does Where We Live and Work Matter?

In this chapter, we'll begin our exploration of the drivers of our productivity and innovation performance by focusing on where our people and industries are. Is economic activity geographically located in rural or urban settings? Are our industries clustered or dispersed? And why are such things important?

Why Do Cities Matter?

The city is emerging as an increasingly important geographic entity, making national and provincial or state boundaries less significant than regional ones in some cases. This increased importance of cities is occurring in spite of the belief of some that information and telecommunications technology advances are making geographic location less significant to economic development. In fact, the opposite is true.

Richard Florida, our colleague at the University of Toronto, has concluded that the world is not getting flatter – it's getting 'spikier.' Linking satellite registration of light-intensity data around the globe to economic activity, he finds that 'the world's ten largest mega-regions in terms of economic activity ... house approximately 6.5% of the world's population, account for 43% of economic activity, 57% of patented technologies, and 53% of the most-cited scientists.'[1] The largest spikes are in North America, Europe, and Japan, while many parts of the world contain valleys with little economic activity. 'The tallest spikes – the cities and regions that drive the world economy – are growing ever higher, while the valleys – places that boast little, if any, economic activity – mostly languish.'[2] And, according to University of Toronto geographer Meric Gertler, 'given the already established centrality of cities to the current and future prosperity of the country, then all the great social policy questions of the day – education, health, poverty, housing and immigration – become urban policy questions.'[3]

Increasing urbanization is a positive portent for Canada's economic prosperity, in that it has been linked to economic growth in several ways:

- *Cities are centres of economic activity.* The 681 metropolitan areas with more than 500,000 people account for a quarter of the world's population but nearly 60 per cent of economic activity.[4] While many economic historians see a progression from rural villages to cities to nation-states, some have concluded that economic activity has always originated in cities.[5]
- *Cities are more productive.* As far back as Adam Smith in 1776 and Alfred Marshall in 1890, economists have theorized that firms and workers are more productive in larger cities. Recently, a team of economists drawing on data from France established this empirically, concluding that a 2 to 8 per cent productivity increase comes from a doubling of city size.[6] Harvard economist Ed Glaeser maintains that in the United States per-capita productivity increases as population density increases.[7]
- *Cities foster innovation.* Not only do cities help lower costs and improve productivity, they provide a natural environment for new ideas. The interaction of highly skilled people, competitive businesses, and sophisticated institutions found in cities can spur innovation. Researchers have concluded that higher density in a metropolitan area – more jobs per square mile – leads to more patents per capita.[8] Glaeser has observed that, while improved transportation and communication have led to the decline of older manufacturing cities as production is shifted offshore, the free flow of ideas in cities makes them natural hubs for innovation. In an information-intensive

economy, this feature will become an even more prominent advantage for cities.[9] As Jane Jacobs noted, cities speed the flow of ideas to stimulate innovation.[10]

- Cities are centres of knowledge and creativity. Richard Florida has observed that innovative people choose to live in areas with the high level of cultural diversity that only cities can offer. Indeed, innovation has been linked to high numbers of foreign-born residents and of musicians and actors, as well as to high levels of tolerance for diversity.[11] University of Toronto political scientists David Wolfe and Alison Bramwell conclude that urban density is critical for knowledge spillovers and innovation.[12] Ed Glaeser and David Mare[13] have found evidence that skills accumulate faster in metropolitan areas, while Glaeser and Matthew Resseger argue that learning occurs more effectively in metropolitan areas.[14] Patent experts Adam Jaffe, Manuel Trajtenberg, and Rebecca Henderson observe that patent applications are more likely to cite previous patents that are geographically proximate.[15]
- Cities build 'social capital.'[16] Economic relationships are intertwined with social relationships. Economic researchers have begun to borrow from sociological perspectives to understand how social relationships affect economic growth. In doing so, they advance the notion of social capital, defined as the social networks and norms that facilitate collective action. A region with a high degree of social capital is likely to support effective collaboration between customers and suppliers (and even between competitors). Social networks tend to be conducive to shared ideals, norms, and values, fostering a sense of trust and thereby facilitating economic activity. Trust lubricates the gears of the economic engine. Social capital, therefore, is an important input in economic growth and the concept correlates well with our understanding of what drives the other important benefit related to 'where we work and live' – the clustering of industries.

One measure of urbanization is the degree to which people live in metropolitan areas. In Canada, Statistics Canada identifies 34 Census

Exhibit 18 **Canadians are less likely to live in metropolitan regions and this lowers productivity**

Metropolitan population and labour productivity, 1996–2009

Note: Canadian results adjusted to U.S. MSA definitions.
Source: Institute for Competitiveness & Prosperity analysis based on data from Statistics Canada, 2006 Census; Provincial Economic Accounts; *Labour Force Survey*; U.S. Census Bureau, U.S. Bureau of Economic Analysis, Regional Economic Accounts, U.S. Bureau of Labor Statistics.

Metropolitan Areas (CMAs), and in the United States the Office of Management and Budget identifies 367 Metropolitan Statistical Areas (MSAs). While the definitions are not exactly the same, both use an urban core of 50,000 as a base and include adjacent municipalities that are integrated with the core, using commuting patterns. Across states and provinces, the higher the share of people living in metropolitan areas,[17] the greater is the productivity (Exhibit 18).

Relatively Low Urbanization Is a Significant Contributor to Our Productivity and Prosperity Gaps

Fewer people live in metropolitan areas in Canada than in the United

States, and our relative productivity and prosperity potential are lower. In 2010 this meant that we had a $2,500 per-capita disadvantage against the United States related to our lower level of urbanization. Looked at another way, if Canada and the United States had the same percentage of their populations living in metropolitan areas, our productivity would increase by 5 per cent. This productivity growth would translate into an increase of $2,500 in GDP per capita.

This isn't to say that we need public policies to shift Canadians to urban centres – that's entirely a choice that people make. Further, creativity and productivity can be improved in rural and urban settings alike, and people in all corners of the country are innovative. Nevertheless, urban settings provide a richer environment for innovation and hence prosperity.

How Does Clustering of Industries Matter?

To prosper, Canadians need to be working in firms and industries that can generate high-paying, high-skill jobs. The kinds of firms and industries that increasingly do this are distinctive global competitors, concentrated geographically – our *clustered* industries. As the name implies, these industries tend to co-locate in specific regions and cities. Through specialization, they thrive on serving consumers outside their region.

We're all familiar with the most visible clustered industries – film production in Hollywood, automotive manufacturers in the Great Lakes region of North America, and printing presses in Heidelberg, Germany. Right now, Canada is home to several – our automotive industry in southwestern Ontario, wine in the Niagara region and the Okanagan valley, technology in Waterloo, oil services in Alberta, and entertainment in Montreal and Vancouver, to name a few. The presence of clustered industries in a region has a spillover effect, in that they typically generate opportunities for increased success of the local economy.

Dispersed industries operate in stark contrast to clustered industries. They are found everywhere across the economy, for example, barber shops, retailers, and landscape architects. And, because they tend to serve only their local market, they don't develop economies of scale and are less challenged to be innovative. As a consequence, they have significantly lower productivity and wage levels.

A third industry type, *natural endowment* industries, is located where natural resources are found. This category includes forestry, mining, and agriculture. These are very small industries – accounting for 1.4 per cent of employment in Canada in 2010.

The concentration of people and industries is one of the most powerful of all economic forces. The great economist Alfred Marshall noted the power of clustering or what he called 'industrial districts.' Economists had long understood that industries and economies can and do benefit from 'economies of scale,' but what Marshall discovered is that a similar kind of productivity gains can come from businesses and people that work in a place together.[18] Later, the Nobel prize-winning economist Robert Lucas noted that the knowledge spillovers that come from the clustering of people are the primary mechanism of economic growth and development – an insight that, he insisted, originated in the writings of Jane Jacobs.[19] During the 1980s and 1990s, Harvard professor Michael Porter drew more attention to industry clusters. He identified a locational paradox – even as offshoring and globalization advance, industry clusters have become more concentrated in individual locations.[20]

Clustered industries drive the North American economy. The forty-one key clustered industries Porter identified – what he calls 'traded clusters' – represent 35 per cent of employment in Canada. But they are responsible for much of the country's overall productivity, as measured by higher wages (18 per cent above average wages across the economy), and lead in innovation as measured by patents (74 per cent of patents in Canada come from these clustered industries) (Exhibit 19). Canada does pretty well with the percentage of our workers in clustered industries. Our 35 per cent compares to 27.4 per cent in the United States.

Our Industry Mix Contributes Positively to Our Productivity

Canada benefits from a mix of industries that is more heavily weighted toward clustered industries, and within these clustered industries we

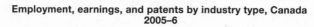

Exhibit 19 **Clustered industries are more productive and innovative**

**Employment, earnings, and patents by industry type, Canada
2005-6**

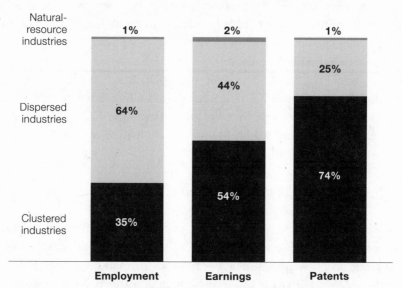

Source: Institute for Competitiveness & Prosperity analysis based on data from Statistics Canada, *Canadian Business Patterns;* Institute for Strategy & Competitiveness, Harvard Business School; U.S. Patent and Trademark Office.

have a more favourable mix for productivity and prosperity than the United States. More Canadians work in clustered industries like financial services, automotive manufacturing, and oil and gas products and services. The potential productivity benefit from this higher percentage of people working in clustered industries is worth $1,900 in GDP per capita. This benefit is derived from a higher value added from our economic activity than would be expected if Canada's mix were the same as that of the United States.

Our Mix of Clustered Industries Also Contributes to Our Productivity

While all clustered industries are positive contributors to productivity and innovation, some have higher potential than others. Canada's relative employment strength in financial services, oil and gas products and services, heavy construction services, entertainment, and others has created an attractive mix of these clustered industries. Our cluster mix accounts for a $1,200 per-capita GDP advantage over the United States. So not only do we have an advantage from having more of our workers in clustered industries; we also have an advantage in the mix of these clustered industries.

But, while we have a relatively high percentage of our workers in the industries that are by their nature productive and innovative, we don't compete effectively in these industries – and hence our productivity and wages trail. We'll discuss our challenges in how effectively we compete in later chapters.

But Aren't We Suffering from Our Lost Manufacturing Base?

Like many of his neighbours, Michael's father worked in manufacturing on an automotive assembly line. Today Michael works in financial services, and few of his neighbours work in manufacturing. It's not because Michael lives in an atypical neighbourhood – it's because so few Canadians hold factory jobs anymore.

In fact, these days it's hard to avoid news about the decline in manufacturing in Canada. With headlines of plant closures and the continuing saga of the auto industry's troubles, it's easy to conclude that all is 'doom and gloom.'

There are some hard data to support this conclusion. To begin with, jobs in the manufacturing sector accounted for about 10 per cent of jobs in Canada in 2011, down from 19 per cent in 1976. Over the 1999–2008 period, manufacturing's share of the economy, as represented by its contribution to the dollar value of GDP, has fallen from about 19 per cent to 12 per cent. On the employment front, manufacturing's share of total employment has also fallen. And the industry has shed more than 300,000 jobs since 2002.

But there is more to these results than meets the eye. In fact, manufacturing employment has held up much better over the past quarter-century in Canada than in other developed economies, including the

United States, Japan, and the United Kingdom. Unlike in these other economies, our manufacturing employment grew dramatically between 1994 and 2004. Part of this was due to the low value of the Canadian dollar over that period. The current weakness is due to the global recession and our stronger dollar. Something that has received less attention is that manufacturing's real output has been growing steadily over the past decades – through employment gains and losses. Factoring in the low price inflation for our manufactured products, the constant dollar value added has actually doubled over the past forty years – as we saw earlier with the experience of the Schmidts through the generations. One benefit is that consumers actually get a lot more for their money when they buy automobiles, food, and telecom products these days than in the past. So we have dramatically increased our manufacturing output with a modest increase in workers. The net effect is a huge increase in real value added per worker – or productivity (Exhibit 20).

Economists and think tanks have long been exhorting our manufacturers to compete on the basis of higher value-added products through more innovation and higher productivity. But many of our manufacturers have actually been doing just that for the past forty years. These include our automotive industry, with global leaders like Husky Injection Molding Systems, whose innovative designs in plastics moulding reduce costs significantly for their customers; and Magna, which has grown to be one of the world's most important automotive-parts companies.

Some smaller, less well-known innovators have also succeeded. Keilhauer Industries, working closely with ergonomics experts, has developed internationally renowned office furniture. Patriot Forge has drawn on technology breakthroughs and skills upgrading to improve its manufacturing process for forging metal. EnerWorks is an innovative solar-thermal technology manufacturer. Gourmet Settings has developed creative designs in stainless steel flatware, as well as streamlining its production process. These firms are succeeding on the basis of innovations in products or processes or both. Some have outsourced manufacturing to lower-wage countries, but they maintain much of their design and marketing work in Canada.

Exhibit 20 **Manufacturing productivity has increased in Canada**

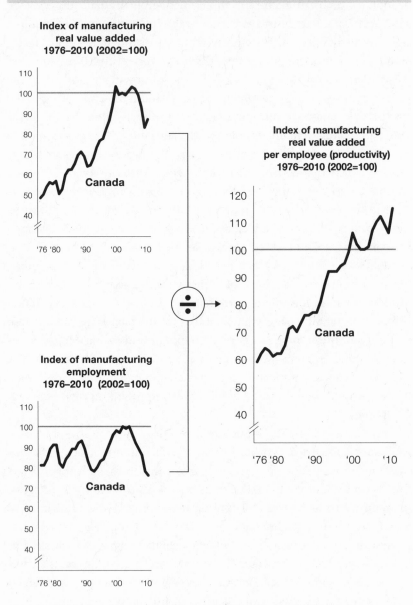

Source: Institute for Competitiveness & Prosperity analysis based on data from Statistics Canada.

In addition, Ontario manufacturers are among the best in the world in the implementation of lean manufacturing, performance management, and people-management initiatives. We need to ensure that our plant-level management strengths are matched by excellence in company leaders who are developing strategies for long-term competitive advantage.

Headlines about plant closures and job losses in manufacturing have alarmed many Canadians, but the reality is mixed. The jobs being shed are the lower-paying ones, and in fact there has been a net increase in high-paying manufacturing jobs.[21] No doubt, however, many high-wage workers in Canadian manufacturing have lost their jobs – and will not find similar compensation in their new employment.

We need innovative public-policy tools to help these workers. One idea worth pursuing is wage insurance – a system that helps fill the wage gap for workers who have to move to a lower-paying job after a plant closure or mass layoff. This may be an effective way to help these workers take on new jobs that enable them to develop new skills. (See sidebar on page 80.)

There is, indeed, much to be concerned about in manufacturing in Canada. Long-term employment growth has trailed that in the rest of the economy. And the recent downturn may have precipitated a real crisis for the industry. Yet, on the positive side, some of Canada's manufacturers have been productivity dynamos. They will have to continue that track record of competing on creativity and skills to survive and thrive. Their success is a model for others to follow to rebuild a vibrant manufacturing sector in Canada that can compete easily in global markets.

The increasing sophistication of our services has contributed mightily to manufacturing productivity. Advances in software and communications services have improved forecasting accuracy for manufacturers and enabled the implementation of just-in-time production, which has reduced waste considerably. Industrial designers have increased efficiency through improved product and process design. New financial products and services have allowed manufacturers to put their

Wage insurance may be the best bet for older displaced workers

Displaced workers face enormous difficulties in attempting to re-enter the workforce. The older the laid-off worker, the greater the subsequent earnings loss. Five
years after a layoff, older workers experienced earnings losses of 40 per cent or
more while younger workers had lower losses and were more likely to reattain their
pre-layoff earnings.

Unfortunately, there is no proven plan to help these displaced workers. Retraining
is the panacea most often promoted. But definitive positive results are hard to come
by.[a]

Wage insurance could be a useful alternative or supplement for workers making
the transition to lower-paid work. It would be targeted at workers who have been in
a job for a period of, say, ten years, with lower benefits for workers with less tenure.
When these workers are re-employed at a lower wage rate, wage-insurance benefits
would cover half the earnings difference for a period of two years. The benefit would
be capped at $10,000. The coverage rate, the coverage period, and the benefit
cap could be adjusted up or down. U.S. calculations of a wage-insurance program
as outlined above indicate a $3.5-billion annual cost, equal to an annual premium of
$25 per worker.

Wage insurance could help ease the hardship that laid-off workers face, particularly older workers with less transportable skills. At the same time, it would motivate
unemployed workers to find a new job; in fact, by reducing the sting of lower wages,
it would encourage them to consider jobs in other sectors where their current skills
are not as valuable. In a sense, wage insurance subsidizes employers to hire and
retrain these workers on the job. It can also assist older workers to remain in the labour force rather than retire early because of poor job prospects at a wage equal to
what they earned before being laid off.

Although the concept of wage insurance is promising, one experiment conducted
in 1995–6 by the federal government's Social Research and Demonstration Corporation yielded disappointing results. The experiment produced only a modest
increase in full-time employment and, after fifteen months, earnings for participants

a   See Institute for Competitiveness & Prosperity, *Report on Canada 2011, Canada's Innovation Imperative*,
    June 2011, 59–60, for a review of the research on the impact of formal retraining programs in Canada and
    the United States.

Exhibit B **Older workers are most severely affected by layoffs**

Average change in earnings for re-employed displaced workers, by age of worker, 1996–2002

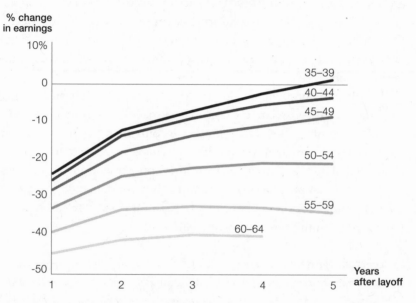

Source: Ross Finnie and David Gray, *Labour-Force Participation of Older Displaced Workers in Canada*, IRPP Study, no. 15, February 2011, Table 5.

were about 5 per cent lower than for those who chose not to join the program.[b] It is possible that better results could come from a redesign of the experiment. There is still much work to be done in assessing the costs and benefits of wage insurance. We would be wise to study the program further.

---

b Howard Bloom, Saul Schwartz, Susanna Lui-Gurr, and Suk-Won Lee, with Jason Pend and Wendy Bancroft, 'Testing a Re-Employment Incentive for Displaced Workers: The Earnings Supplement Project,' Social Research and Demonstration Corporation, May 1999.

---

working capital to better use, thereby making their production more efficient. Advances in health care have reduced absenteeism in manufacturing – and in all industries.

The disaggregation of many industries, especially manufacturing, also contributes to the apparent trend toward services in our economy. When a manufacturer outsources its information-technology work to an IT services provider, official statistics record a decrease in jobs in the goods-producing sector and an increase in the services sector – even though the same people may be doing the very same jobs as before the outsourcing. That is hardly what people think of as a decline in manufacturing jobs.

This phenomenon will accelerate. As Canadians have been growing wealthier, we spend relatively less on basic needs. For example, India's consumers, with a much lower level of income than Canadians, spend 46 per cent of their income on food;[22] Canadians spend only 10 per cent. Moreover, there is only so much furniture, appliances, and automobiles that a family can purchase over a lifetime. But our demand for services – health care, education, financial advice, dining away from home, to name a few – continues to grow unabated.

As we review the issue of where we live and work, we find that these two factors work in opposite directions. Fewer of us live in metropolitan regions than our U.S. counterparts; we still have a higher percentage of our population living in smaller towns and cities and in rural areas. This is a drag on our productivity and innovation – but not something that can be addressed through public policy. Meanwhile, more of us are working in clustered industries, but we do not gain full advantage from them. To do so, we will need to increase our innovative capacity.

5 How Do We Compete?

Canadians are less likely to live in metropolitan areas than Americans, and this is a drag on our productivity and prosperity. We do have an excellent industry mix in Canada – more of our workers are in the highest productivity industries. But do we compete effectively? Do we harness our beneficial mix of clusters and industries to create the right conditions to drive competitiveness and prosperity? The answer is no.

Canada's clustered industries are much less productive than those in the United States. In the same clustered industries, wages in Canadian firms are lower than those of their counterparts in the United States. Across all clustered industries, the average wage in Canada is 21 per cent lower than that in the United States. Lower wages reflect lower productivity and innovation in our clustered industries, which in turn reduce the economic performance of all industries.

If Canada's clusters were as effective as U.S. clusters, annual wages would be $16,100 per worker higher in these industries. As traded clusters account for 34.8 per cent of Canadian employment, our overall productivity would rise by 13.4 per cent.[1] From this, we estimate the productivity loss from the lower effectiveness of our clusters to be $5,100 per capita.

This relative ineffectiveness in how we compete is at the heart of our lost potential in Canada. It is not the result of an attitudinal deficit; rather, we have not created the best context for competitiveness in Canada.

Exhibit 21 **Our attitudes support innovation and risk taking**

Ontarians agree slightly more than peer U.S. state citizens, managers, and business leaders with the following statements:

'People who start their own businesses deserve all the money they make'

'When businesses do well, we all win'

'Business is the most important contributor to prosperity'

'Competition between businesses is a good thing'

'Being globally competitive makes a firm stronger'

Source: Institute for Competitiveness & Prosperity, *Striking similarities: Attitudes and Ontario's prosperity gap*, September 2003.

While we relish competition, risk, and innovation, we don't translate these attitudes into actions.

Attitudes toward Innovation Are Positive but Do Not Lead to Action

Attitudes that lead to high aspirations, self-confidence, the desire to succeed, an entrepreneurial spirit, and creativity are important drivers of economic success. It is received wisdom that Canadians don't have the same attitudes toward prosperity, competitiveness, and innovation as our U.S. counterparts. But the evidence for this 'shortcoming' is non-existent. This is one of those myths that get in the way of sound economic policy in Canada.

Based on our research comparing Ontarians with residents of large U.S. states, we conclude that Canadians do not have a fundamentally different outlook from our American counterparts on many aspects of competitiveness. Attitudinal differences between the public and businesses in Canada and the United States are not significant roadblocks to closing the prosperity gap.[2] In contrast to commonly held perceptions, we differ very little from our counterparts in how we view business and business leaders, risk and success, and competition and competitiveness (Exhibit 21).

We're not the only ones who have found this attitude myth to be unfounded. The Expert Panel on Business Innovation observes that there is a widespread conviction in the Canadian business community that there is a deficiency of ambition within its ranks. Yet it could find no hard, quantitative evidence that supported this view. The shortage of global competitors from Canada 'is not due to any lack of innate capacities of business people – it is not in the "DNA" so to speak. Rather, the traditional attitudes of business people have been shaped over a very long time by particular circumstances of Canada's economy.'[3] These circumstances include easy access to the large U.S. market, limited domestic competition, the smallness of our domestic market, and inertia stemming from our traditional success.

If anything is 'wrong' with our attitudes in Canada, it may be that we are complacent about the impact of our prosperity gap. Canadians show little concern about a prosperity gap with the United States until they are informed about the impact on their standard of living.[4] It is likely that our complacency derives from our ignorance of the existence and magnitude of the prosperity gap.

Deloitte Canada conducted some original research in 2011 on attitudinal differences between Canadian and American business leaders. [5] Like us, it found that business leaders report similar levels of tolerance for the kind of risk associated with growth and innovation. But it is also easier to avoid risk taking in Canada. Deloitte dug deeper in its research to measure risk tolerance by the actual decisions businesses reported making and how these decisions were made. Based on the responses, Deloitte divided executives into two groups – those who were 'risk takers' and those who were 'risk avoiders.' Canadian and American executives split in about the same proportions. The proportion of risk takers participating in R&D was about the same in the two countries. But risk avoiders in the United States were more likely to participate in R&D activities than risk avoiders in Canada. This difference accounts for most of the lower rate of R&D participation in Canada. Deloitte found similar patterns in the areas of commercialization of innovation, how risk is measured, and dependence on government for support of innovation.

It seems that risk avoiders among Canada's business leaders are less likely to pursue risks associated with growth and innovation than risk avoiders in the United States. In fact, U.S. risk avoiders are as likely as risk takers to pursue risk. It appears to us that there is more hiding room in Canada for executives preferring a comfortable, low- risk environment. It's not fundamentally different attitudes in the two countries – it's the context for competition. For us, this inability to translate positive attitudes into actions is because we lack competitive intensity and sophisticated support structures.

As Kevin Schmidt was growing up, he exhibited a great talent for hockey. As a youngster he was a fast skater and as he got bigger and stronger, he developed a wicked slapshot. Naturally, his father saw National Hockey League (NHL) potential and did everything he could to support the dream. Kevin started out in house league at age six and led his team in scoring. At age nine, he had the opportunity to try out for the 'select' team – made up of the best players in house league chosen by the coaches (in house league all registrants are assigned to a team and have equal playing time). He made the team and was a standout in the league, which had teams from neighbouring communities outside Burlington. The select team had frequent practices and coaches who helped develop specialized skills, such as skating, passing, play making, and shooting. At first, Kevin was a little overwhelmed by the higher level of competition he now faced. Goals didn't come so easily as he was opposed by players with much higher skill levels than those he faced in house league. He also noticed that his teammates were not always looking to pass the puck to him since he wasn't the only goal-scoring threat. But, with more practice and determination, Kevin became one of the top players on the select team.

At age thirteen, Kevin was asked to try out for the Bantam AA Burlington Eagles. What sold him and his parents on the benefits of joining this team was the opportunity to develop the skills necessary to compete at the very highest levels as he grew older. Kevin made the team, and was one step closer to his dream. This was also a big step for Michael and Maria because they would be travelling even more to hockey games – more frequently and longer distances. Kevin started off well with the Eagles and his father was already thinking about his son's first game with his favourite NHL team, the Edmonton Oilers.

Kevin's next step would be to make the AAA team, the highest level for fifteen- and sixteen-year-olds. From this level, the Ontario Hockey League (OHL) drafts its players. Making the OHL by age seventeen would place Kevin among the elite players in the world and make him a candidate to be drafted by a NHL team at age eighteen. However, Kevin couldn't get past AA – it was as far as he could go. It was a difficult realization, especially for Michael. But before too long, Kevin joined his high school team and went back to playing house-league hockey with his friends.

Kevin's cousin had a much different experience. The two started together in house-league hockey when they were six, and it was hard to determine who was the better player. Nor was it obvious which of the two had the drive to excel. Michael and his brother-in-law had their opinions, but they didn't share them with each other. They'll never really know because Kevin's cousin and his family moved to Atlanta when he was seven. He joined a house-league hockey team and led his team in scoring. He was on the all-star team for his league and travelled a bit to tournaments and friendly matches – but experienced nothing like the intense competition and skills-development support that Kevin had. From time to time, Kevin's uncle dreamed about moving back to Canada so that his son would have the same hockey opportunities and challenges as Kevin. Atlanta just didn't have as many rinks for games and practices, nor the expert coaches, nor the competitive intensity.

This is a metaphor for our competitive environment in Canada. Our businesses operate in the Atlanta of this story. We believe that our business leaders are as capable as their U.S. counterparts. They aren't fundamentally different when it comes to attitudes toward risk and innovation. But we have smaller markets, and this in turn means that our industries have less competitive intensity. It also means that we have less sophisticated and specialized support in education and ancillary industries like legal services or investment banks.

To compensate, Canada needs to find opportunities to intensify competition and gain access to the highest levels of specialized support. Free trade and foreign direct investment (FDI) are part of the answer. Finding innovative ways to enhance the capabilities of our managers is another. It doesn't help that we still have wide swaths of our industries where regulations protect the participants from intense domestic and foreign competition – health care, communications, publishing, and transportation, to name a few. For us, it is a question of what can bring out and accentuate the creative capacity that is inherent in Canada.

We Aren't Competing on Creativity

Earlier, we reviewed the different kinds of industries in an economy as defined by Michael Porter. Another way to understand an economy is to look at the occupations people are in. Richard Florida's analysis of the occupational classes is the most commonly used approach.

Two basic types of occupations are found in our economy – creativity-oriented and routine-oriented occupations. *Creativity-oriented* occupations (Florida's 'creative class') demand that workers apply thinking skills and knowledge to changing situations and make decisions on how best to proceed. These occupations require the worker to explore possibilities to reach a feasible solution to an issue. An experienced lawyer, for example, will recognize the key problems in a case and determine what tasks need to be done in what order for that specific case. But every lawyer's case is different. Creativity-oriented jobs call for knowledge and understanding in specific fields, but they also depend heavily on the ability of workers to recognize patterns, analyze alternatives, and decide the best way to proceed. Creativity-oriented jobs include scientists and technologists, artists and entertainers, and managers and analysts.

Routine-oriented occupations require workers to carry out tasks in a prescribed order or to do the same tasks repetitively according to a preordained set of operating procedures. In essence, they follow a specific set of procedures that will produce the desired result, as exemplified by the typical assembly-line job originated by Henry Ford where workers are explicitly asked not to use their judgment or creativity. Some

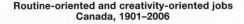

Exhibit 22 **The share of creativity-oriented jobs is increasing**

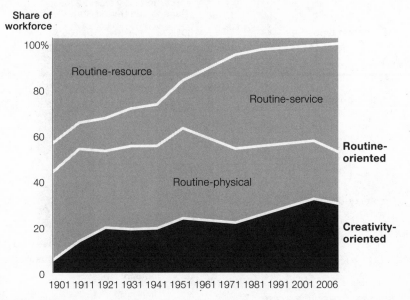

Routine-oriented and creativity-oriented jobs
Canada, 1901–2006

Share of
workforce

Routine-resource

Routine-service

Routine-
oriented

Routine-physical

Creativity-
oriented

100%

80

60

40

20

0

1901 1911 1921 1931 1941 1951 1961 1971 1981 1991 2001 2006

Note: The 1961 and 1991 data points have been approximated owing to data limitations.
Source: Martin Prosperity Institute analysis based on data from Statistics Canada.

routine-oriented jobs have a large physical element to them. But the greatest proportion of routine-oriented jobs today is found in service occupations – such as servers who follow standard procedures in restaurants and clerical staff who do likewise with paperwork.

It is clear that there is a spectrum in jobs running from the most creativity-oriented to the most routine-oriented and it isn't an exact science to define the dividing line. However, it is possible to rank job classifications on the basis of the judgment and decision-making required to come up with the proportion of creativity-oriented versus routine-oriented jobs.

The proportion of people performing creativity-oriented work in occupations has increased threefold over the past century and especially over the past two decades (Exhibit 22). But today even the most routine job calls for more creativity than in the past.

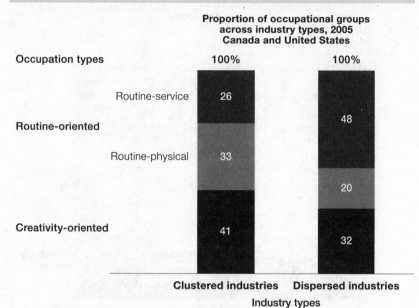

Exhibit 23 **Clustered industries draw more on creativity-oriented occupations**

Proportion of occupational groups across industry types, 2005 Canada and United States

Occupation types

	Clustered industries	Dispersed industries
Routine-service	26	48
Routine-physical	33	20
Creativity-oriented	41	32

Routine-oriented

Creativity-oriented

Clustered industries   Dispersed industries

Industry types

Note: Full-time and part-time combined.
Source: Martin Prosperity Institute and Institute for Competitiveness & Prosperity analysis based on data from Statistics Canada; U.S. Census Bureau, American Community Survey, County Business Patterns.

While creativity increases economic growth, and clusters increase productivity, it's instructive to look at the combined effects of creative occupations and clustered industries to understand our economy better. This is the first effort, to our knowledge, to examine a region's economy through two lenses – industries and occupations: what firms produce and what workers do.

The implications for an advanced economy like Canada's are striking. Clustered industries are more likely to draw on creativity-oriented occupations (Exhibit 23). This is because these industries compete on productivity and value-added innovation and are more likely to be challenged to upgrade continuously by global competitors. Those in routine-oriented physical occupations are also more likely to be

Exhibit 24 **Creativity-oriented clusters generate higher earnings**

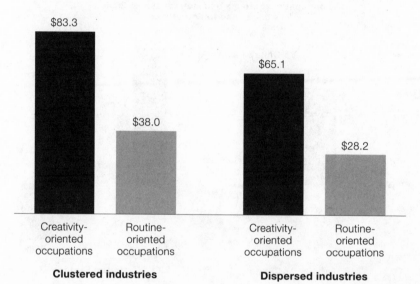

Average employment income, Canada and United States
(000 C$2005)

$83.3

$65.1

$38.0

$28.2

| Creativity-oriented occupations | Routine-oriented occupations | Creativity-oriented occupations | Routine-oriented occupations |
| **Clustered industries** | | **Dispersed industries** | |

Note: Currency converted at PPP; full-time and part-time combined; 18 years old and above.
Source: Martin Prosperity Institute and Institute for Competitiveness & Prosperity analysis based on data from Statistics Canada; U.S. Census Bureau, American Community Survey, County Business Patterns.

employed in clustered industries. This is driven largely by the need for successful manufacturers to achieve scale to compete effectively.

Workers in routine-oriented service occupations are more likely to be employed in dispersed industries. Many of these industries are primarily local-service providers, like restaurants and retailers, and they rely more on face-to-face or personal service.

Wages are dramatically higher for workers in creativity-oriented occupations in clustered industries – more than twice as high as those in routine-oriented occupations and about 28 per cent higher than those in creativity-oriented dispersed industries (Exhibit 24).

But Canadians' wages lag our U.S. peers' wages. The premium paid to

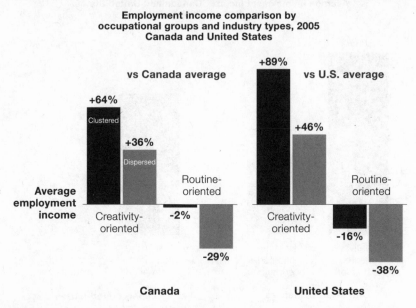

Exhibit 25 **Wage differences between occupational and industry groups are much less prevalent in Canada than the United States**

Employment income comparison by occupational groups and industry types, 2005 Canada and United States

Note: Full-time and part-time combined; 18 years old or above.
Source: Canadian Census, 2006, Canadian Business Patterns, 2006, Statistics Canada, Table 380–0057, Martin Prosperity Institute and Institute for Competitiveness & Prosperity analysis based on data from American Community Survey, PUMS 2005, County Business Patterns, 2005.

our workers in creativity-oriented occupations versus those in routine-oriented occupations is much lower than that in the United States. And the premium paid to workers in creativity-oriented occupations in our clustered industries versus their counterparts in dispersed industries is also lower than that in the United States (Exhibit 25). In Canada, creativity-oriented occupations in clustered industries generate earnings that are 64 per cent above the national average, which sounds good until you consider that the premium is a whopping 89 per cent in the United States.

Furthermore, our clustered industries do not have the same level of creativity-oriented occupations as those in the United States. As we have seen, Canada has more workers in clustered industries and this should provide a productivity advantage. However, we dissipate that advantage by operating these industries with less creativity content. When we examine the occupations of workers in our clustered industries, we find that the percentage who are creativity-oriented is lower in Canada than the United States.

We must increase the creativity content of all our occupations and industries. The increased efficiency that comes from better job design along with greater use of technology and better management will make these occupations more efficient and thus require fewer workers. This will allow for a shift in employment from dispersed industries to clustered industries. At the same time, we must encourage the development of more creativity-oriented occupations in clustered industries.

We Haven't Achieved the Right Balance of Support and Pressure

Specialized support and competitive pressure drive productivity, innovation, and prosperity (Exhibit 26). Specialized support from skilled workers and managers, government support for R&D, capable suppliers, and related industries push innovation higher in all industries, particularly clustered ones. At the same time, more competitive pressure from sophisticated customers and vigorous rivals drives innovation. Our innovation system in Canada has not achieved the right balance of support and pressure.

Two points of clarification are in order:

- *Support* refers to the conditions that provide a foundation of assistance to all firms and individuals as they compete and develop. Typical support elements include the availability of capital to entrepreneurs, well-educated and skilled workers, specialized suppliers of goods and services, easy access to markets, and excellent infrastructure.
- *Pressure* comes from aggressive and capable competitors, who threaten complacency, and from sophisticated customers, who demand innovative goods and services at low prices.

Exhibit 26 **Support and pressure drive innovation**

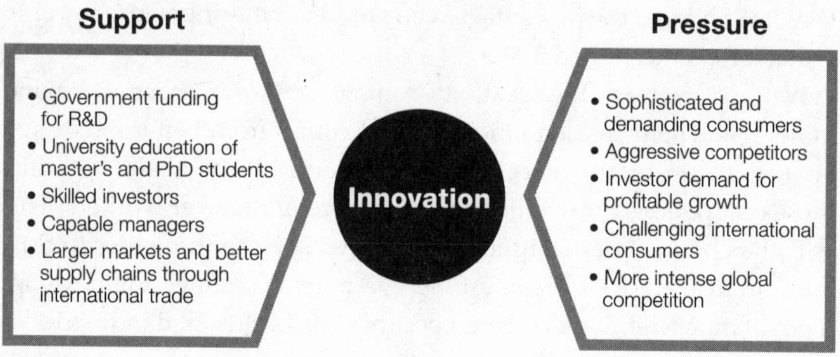

Support   **Pressure**

- Government funding
  for R&D
- University education of
  master's and PhD students
- Skilled investors
- Capable managers
- Larger markets and better
  supply chains through
  international trade

Innovation

- Sophisticated and
  demanding consumers
- Aggressive competitors
- Investor demand for
  profitable growth
- Challenging international
  consumers
- More intense global
  competition

Source: Institute for Competitiveness & Prosperity.

These two drivers of higher productivity and continuous innovation in an economy need to work in balance – both have to be present. Each element of the economy needs to have not only support to make its task easier but also pressure to provide incentives to move ahead. All support and no pressure creates a comfortable and lazy environment inimical to productivity and innovation. All pressure and no support creates a harsh and barren environment, equally inimical to productivity and innovation.

Higher productivity and innovation result in product and process upgrades across the entire economy. But, if one element of the economy lacks the necessary support or pressure, then the whole system will not perform to its potential. Having an imposing strength in one element will not make up for weakness in another.

As we describe throughout this book, Canada lacks specialized support and competitive pressure in several areas:

- We trail the United States in the percentage of our population with university degrees. More highly educated workers are more innovative and productive. Our gap is higher for graduate degrees than for bachelor's degrees. This lowers the level of specialized *support* for our businesses to achieve innovation.

- This education gap is even more pronounced among mangers, another way in which our businesses lack the *support* for innovation. In our clustered manufacturing industries, we have evidence that Canada has a lower level of management capability than the United States.
- For more than a century, Canada protected our industries from foreign competition, thus reducing the *pressure* from competitive intensity. We've had free trade for a quarter-century now, but many industries still don't face full-on competition.[6] The demand conditions for our clustered industries are not as sophisticated as those in the United States.[7]

We don't compete as effectively as we could in Canada. It's not because we're nice people who don't like to compete or take risks. We have the attitudes to succeed. Instead, we haven't created the environment for sophisticated economic activity in Canada. Our businesses and individuals operate at a lower level of competitive intensity than their U.S. counterparts. As a result, we are not investing adequately in ourselves and our businesses.

6 How Do We Invest?

How effectively we compete is very much driven by how much we invest in ourselves and our physical capital. In turn, people and businesses that are competing more effectively have a greater propensity to invest. Individuals, businesses, and governments must invest to ensure future growth and prosperity. That investment comes at the expense of current consumption. Thus, the balance between current consumption and future investment is critical. In the important areas of investment in post-secondary education and in machinery and equipment, Canada has under-invested dramatically.

Investment and Consumption Need to Be in Balance

With the benefits of prosperity generated from past investments, individuals, businesses, and governments can choose between two paths: invest for tomorrow or consume today. The underlying logic for the consumption path is that prosperity will continue at an adequate level without investing in it, and that we should enjoy our prosperity to the maximum today. The underlying logic for the investment path is that investing today and forgoing some consumption of current prosperity will create even higher prosperity down the road.

In one sense, these are the often tough choices that all societies must make. But in another sense, investment is a means to an end – future prosperity – that will enable jurisdictions to achieve their goal of higher future consumption. Setting aside a judicious portion of current prosperity for investment will increase future prosperity, which will then sustain greater future consumption as well as the capacity for robust future investment.

The balance between the two is important. Societies that over-invest at the expense of consumption run the risk of losing social cohesion. This is a current challenge for China where the leadership has to balance its desire to invest in infrastructure with its people's desire to enjoy the fruits of their labour.[1] But societies that over-consume and under-invest do not create the conditions for increased future prosperity. By doing so, they constrain their ability to increase consumption in the future. Worse, their capacity for future investment will be lower, because they are less prosperous.

Investment can take many forms – investing in upgrading people's skills or investing in capital goods for business and government services. Fundamentally, investment is a means to generate future prosperity. Consumption can also take many forms – for individuals, it can be the extra vacation; for businesses, it can be greater community involvement; for governments, it can mean higher spending on social services. But, fundamentally, consumption is the benefit of prosperity.

Like others, Canadians need to invest in their future prosperity – and that requires forgoing some current consumption. Some expenditures are pure investment – that is, completely forgoing current benefit for the prospect of long-term prosperity. Investment in machinery and equipment, R&D, and retirement savings are examples. Very few expenditures are pure consumption, however; many are a mixture of consumption and investment. For example, when the Schmidts take a vacation, that consumes some of their current prosperity, yet the family's leisure time can recharge their energy and ultimately make Michael and Maria more productive at their jobs.

A jurisdiction that under-invests slowly erodes the relative strength of its human skills and capital stock compared to other advanced and advancing economies. This erosion in turn reduces the productivity of its workers and hence its competitiveness and prosperity. Without the most sophisticated skills and capital support, workers are limited in how much they can increase their productivity. This limits wages.

Health care is an interesting and complicated mix of consumption and investment. In many respects, it is a prototypical consumption item; societies that are sufficiently prosperous can afford to provide the benefit of health care to all citizens. Perhaps the most pure form of heath-care consumption is care for retired citizens. However, care that enables a child who would otherwise never enter the workforce to get a job and work for forty years is an investment; there is zero economic payoff today, but huge payoff in the future.

The Schmidts have benefited greatly from Canada's health-care system. Maria gave birth to three happy and healthy babies in world-class hospitals with excellent medical care. As Michael's and Maria's grandparents aged, they also received excellent care. Nobody doubts the importance of this kind of consumption spending.

The important point is that consumption and investment spending are not fundamentally opposed to each other but, in fact, complementary. Investment spending is a means to an end, and consumption spending is the end goal of prosperity.

Canada has clearly been on the consumption path. And that is hurting our prosperity. We need to change course.

Education Is Investment

Traditionally, the inputs for economic growth have been understood to be capital and labour. But economists now conclude that knowledge plays a critical role in economic growth. Human capital – the ideas, skills, and expertise of people – is a fundamental input into the economic process. Investment in the post-secondary education of the workforce is therefore a fundamental driver of economic growth.[2]

Studies show repeatedly that individuals' earnings increase with their level of education (Exhibit 27). In fact, the best single predictor of personal income is level of education. The most valuable advice parents

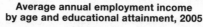

Exhibit 27 **More education means higher earnings**

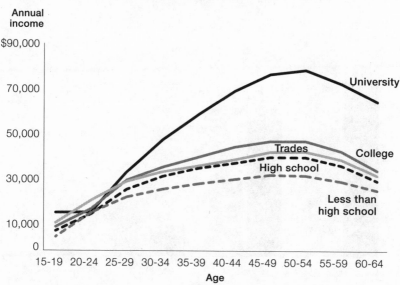

**Average annual employment income
by age and educational attainment, 2005**

Source: Statistics Canada, 2006 Census of Population and Council of Ministers of Education, Education Indicators in *Canada: Report of the Pan-Canadian Education Indicators Program, 2005*, Catalogue no. 81–582–XIE.

can give their children is to stay in school. As we'll see, those with less education, particularly less than a high school diploma, are more likely to do poorly economically and actually experience poverty.

And society as a whole, not just individuals, benefits from investment in post-secondary education. For one thing, a more educated and better-trained labour force creates more value. In addition, universities' research benefits spill over to local communities in the regional innovation system. A healthy symbiosis develops as businesses draw on research from universities, and this helps guide researchers in their future work. Besides providing for a better-educated workforce, spending on post-secondary education has been positively correlated with both innovation and high-technology industrial activity.[3]

A better-educated workforce will be more productive. Education

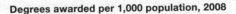

Exhibit 28 **Fewer degrees are awarded in Canada than in the United States, especially at the master's level**

Degrees awarded per 1,000 population, 2008

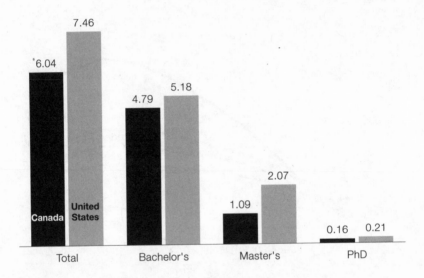

Note: Calendar year 2008 for Canada. Academic year 2007–8 for United States.
Source: Institute for Competitiveness & Prosperity analysis based on data from Association of Universities & Colleges of Canada, U.S. Department of Education, National Center for Education Statistics.

increases workers' base level of knowledge necessary for improved job performance. It increases workers' flexibility so that they are able to gain new skills throughout their lifetimes. Higher wages accrue to more highly educated individuals. And higher wages are the result of higher productivity.

Yet Canadians are under-investing in achieving university degrees (Exhibit 28).

Canada's population has, on average, a lower level of educational attainment compared to those living in the United States, particularly for university graduates. Adjusting the mix of educational attainment in Canada to match that of the United States and holding wages constant at each attainment level, Canada's productivity would be higher by $1,900 per capita.

Michael's formal education has enabled him to advance through the bank – contributing more every year to its success and earning more for himself and his family. While his university degree is in English, he developed the foundations for ongoing learning throughout his life so that he could comprehend the concepts in computer systems, and this has allowed him to become a highly respected systems analyst at the bank. While at school, Michael developed the confidence that he could take on new intellectual challenges and the learning habits to master them. He took every opportunity the bank offered him for training in the bank's computer systems – forgoing leisure time in the evenings and on weekends to attend courses and study. Many of Michael's high school classmates couldn't wait to receive their high school diploma and get that first factory or mill job that paid so well. In the early years of his career, Michael's paycheque was smaller and he sometimes wondered if getting that English degree was worth it. But gradually, his career advanced and he was earning more than most of his high school classmates. He also noticed that some of his friends went through stretches of unemployment, which never really was a threat for him.

Michael and Maria realized the importance of education for their children, and it was always understood at the Schmidt home that the children would not stop at a high school diploma. Parents have a really important effect on whether their children go to university. Children whose parents went to university are much more likely to attend university themselves; if parents have stressed the importance of post-secondary education, children are much more likely to attend university.[4] Consequently, the Schmidts' daughter Sandra went to university to get a degree in biology, although she interrupted her studies to have a baby. Kevin earned an undergraduate degree in economics and plans on pursuing his MBA. Louise hasn't made up her mind yet, but is sure that she will be heading off to college or university education after high school.

The Shift to Health-Care Spending Is Consumption

To the extent we are willing to defer some current consumption to fund investments in our future, we will be building an ongoing base for improving our capabilities to upgrade. We are not talking about a puritanical notion that we should not enjoy the fruits of our current prosperity. In fact, the vast majority of our prosperity is for today's consumption.

A clear example of the need to increase investments in our future is our lagging *public expenditure* in education. Comparing our current public spending patterns in Canada with those in the previous decade and in the United States, we find that we are falling behind. As recently as 1992, all levels of government across Canada spent $2,500 per capita on education (in 2009 dollars) – 4.4 per cent more than we spent on health care (Exhibit 29). Subsequently, however, this figure fell sharply.

In 1992, investment in education was not on many Canadians' radar screens. Instead, our attention was focused on debt and deficits. Federally, the deficit had ballooned from $1 billion in 1971 to $33 billion in 1984. Despite the concern expressed by the new federal government, annual budget deficits remained standard practice, and by 1992–3 the deficit had tipped over the $40-billion mark. When Standard & Poor's (S&P) downgraded Canada's credit rating, the federal and provincial governments owed $665 billion among them, about $300 billion of which was foreign debt. The total amounted to over 96 per cent of the country's GDP, while in the United States national debt was only 66 per cent.[5]

Then, over the two fiscal years between 1995–6 and 1997–8, the federal government achieved an impressive $33-billion turnaround in Ottawa's fiscal position, moving from a $30-billion deficit to a $3-billion surplus. The economy had helped by providing $21 billion of that figure in increased revenues, but the government also cut $12 billion in federal spending. By 1997–8, the federal government was in surplus, a task thought five years earlier to be impossible.

But where did the federal government find that $12 billion in cuts? The biggest rollback was in transfers to the provinces – money used to fund education and health care, the two biggest provincial expenditures. Ottawa chopped almost $8 billion, or 24 per cent, from this budget line between 1995–6 and 1997–8, a time when the provinces were all dealing with their own fiscal challenges. By 1999–2000, provincial

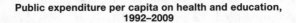

Exhibit 29 **Since 1996, public investment in education in Canada has trailed U.S. spending significantly**

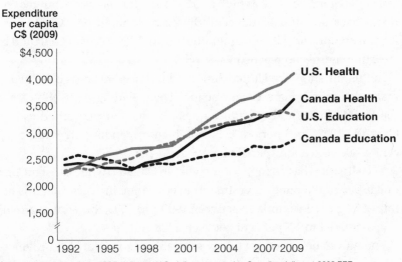

Public expenditure per capita on health and education, 1992–2009

Expenditure
per capita
C$ (2009)

U.S. Health

Canada Health

U.S. Education

Canada Education

Notes: Values deflated using GDP deflators. U.S. dollars converted to Canadian dollars at 2009 PPP.
Source: Institute for Competitiveness & Prosperity analysis based on data from Statistics Canada, Consolidated Government Revenue and Expenditures; U.S. Census Bureau, State and Local Government Finances; Office of Management and Budget, Historical Tables; National Academy of Social Insurance, *Workers' Compensation: Benefits, Coverage, and Costs, 2008.*

transfers were nearly back to the level they were at in 1995–6. But by then the provinces had already changed their approaches to spending.

As governments at both levels tackled deficits, they cut real per-capita spending on education at a much faster rate than that on health-care spending. By 1998, governments in Canada were spending more on health care than on education. This gap continued to widen considerably, as health-care spending per capita increased at an annual trend-line real rate of 3.6 per cent between 1998 and 2009, while education spending increased only 1.6 per cent annually. In 2009 per-capita public spending on health care outpaced spending on education by 27 per cent. In effect, governments spent more on health-care consumption than on investment in education (Exhibit 29).

Contrast our response to the 1990–3 economic downturn with that of the United States, which admittedly entered the recession in better fiscal shape than Canada. Total deficits across all levels of government there represented 4.2 per cent of GDP in 1990, before the recession struck. That figure grew as high as 5.8 during the recession, but by 1995 it was back down to 3.1 per cent. By comparison, in 1990 Canada had federal and provincial deficits amounting to 5.8 per cent of GDP, and by 1992 that figure had reached 9 per cent.

In this situation, the United States did not need to engage in the dramatic deficit fighting seen in Canada. The spending on health care in the United States did not grow much faster than that on education. Over the 1992–2009 period, U.S. health-care spending grew at 3.6 per cent while education spending grew at 2.7 per cent.

The situation has changed somewhat in Canada; while constant 2009 dollar per-capita public investments in education increased slightly at a rate of 1.5 per cent annually between 1997 and 2005, this annual growth rate increased to 1.8 per cent between 2005 and 2009.

The gap to be closed is still considerable. As federal and provincial governments have turned their attention to the massive deficits they generated since 2009, they need to ensure that spending cuts are made appropriately and with the long term in mind. Investment in education has a significant impact on the economy.

Acquisition of Physical Assets and Technology Is Investment

Another critical area of investment is the acquisition of new physical assets or refurbishment of existing ones. This investment – in machinery, equipment, software, and non-residential infrastructure – enables workers to be more productive, giving them newer and better tools to do their work.

Innovation and upgrading of products, services, and production processes are typically embedded in the machinery and equipment component of investment. Increasingly, this investment consists of computer hardware and software and telecommunications made by knowledge-intensive companies – a key driver of productivity growth. There is a positive and statistically significant relationship between investment in machinery and equipment and growth in GDP per worker.[6]

Michael Schmidt's job focuses on providing workers and organizations with the technology to improve their productivity. At his bank, as at other Canadian banks and banks around the world, technology is becoming more and more important. Michael helps evaluate and implement the newest software to improve security, thereby enabling new credit-card products and more Internet-banking features. He and his bank know that, unless they are applying the most advanced, reliable technology to their business, the bank will slowly lose customers.

The other Schmidts have and will continue to benefit from technology. Maria was able to upgrade her teaching credentials through distance learning, thanks to investments in hardware and software by her university. Maria's father benefited from advanced machinery and technology in the construction industry. One innovation was the development of better cement mixers and containers to support the introduction of ready-mix concrete, which allows for mixing concrete away from the construction site but customizing it to the requirements for each site. This innovation saved time, space, and costs. Other innovations, from nail guns to tower cranes, have helped the construction industry achieve productivity gains. In fact, the construction industry experienced above-average productivity gains over the period from 1997 to 2007, and capital investments were an important contributor. During those same years, employment in the industry grew by more than 350,000 workers – or 50 per cent.[7]

In fact, the impact of machinery and equipment investment on output growth is about four times higher than the impact of other capital investments.[8] In 1999 economist Pierre Fortin noted that lower investment in machinery and equipment in Canada relative to the United States was a principal reason for the growing productivity gap between the two countries.[9]

Canadian businesses have under-invested in machinery, equipment, and software relative to their counterparts in the United States, so that the capital base that supports workers in Canada is not as modern as that of their counterparts south of the border. As a result, Canadian workers are not as productive. This under-investment in capital equipment lowers Canada's productivity by $500 per capita, an estimate based on our simulation of Canada's GDP if we had matched the rate at which the U.S. private sector invested in machinery, equipment, and software.[10]

Investments that are made are typically allocated to information and communications technology (ICT) and to all other categories, such as transportation equipment and traditional factory equipment. ICT accounts for about a third of investment in machinery, equipment, and software. And our major gap is in ICT investment.

On a per-worker basis, U.S. businesses out-invest Canadian businesses in machinery and equipment overall, with the gap being larger in ICT (Exhibit 30). True, since much of machinery and equipment is imported, the strengthening of the Canadian dollar has been an advantage for our businesses. Consequently, the gap between Canada and U.S. investment per worker began to narrow in 2005. However, the gap has widened again recently. In 1987 our businesses invested 21 per cent less per worker in all machinery, equipment, and software; in 2001 this gap had grown to 31 per cent.

In 2010 the Canada-U.S. gap in ICT investment per worker was $2,000 or 45 per cent, while in other machinery and equipment the gap was $900 or 17 per cent. The accumulated effect of this under-investment by Canadian businesses each year means that their workers have less capital to support them on the job.

Further exploration of ICT expenditures reveals that the major source of our investment gap is in the area of software, with a smaller gap in computer hardware and telecommunications equipment. It appears that Canadian businesses have a higher propensity to purchase hardware, which tends more to be off-the-shelf, than to acquire software, which can be customized to specific business processes. This is one more example of our businesses attenuating their investment profile. We invest in the basics but lag in the more sophisticated elements that are part of our innovative strategies.

Exhibit 30 **Canadian businesses lag their U.S. counterparts in ICT investments, especially software**

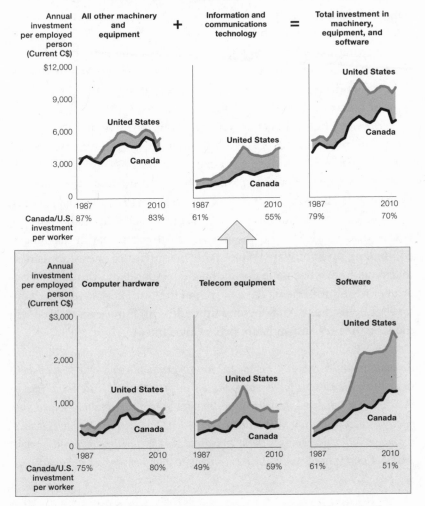

Private-sector machinery, equipment, and software investment, 1987–2010

Note: U.S. dollars converted to Canadian dollars using PPP for M&E. The 2010 PPP for M&E is estimated based on CAD/USD exchange rates.
Source: Institute for Competitiveness & Prosperity analysis based on data from Statistics Canada (special tabulations); Labour Force Survey; Centre for Study of Living Standards Database of Information and Communication Technology (ICT), Investment and Capital Stock Trends: Canada vs United States, http://www.csls.ca/data/ict.asp; U.S. Department of Commerce, Bureau of Economic Analysis; U.S. Census Bureau, U.S. Bureau of Labor Statistics, Current Population Survey.

Closing the investment gap offers the potential for closing the prosperity gap. With more machinery, equipment, and software investment, our workforce could be more productive. And investment in ICT enhances productivity at three levels. At the most basic level, equipping staff with computers and software increases firm and national productivity. At the second level, connecting computers in networks and drawing on more technologies can drive productivity even higher. But the most significant benefit of ICT adoption can be that it enables the profound transformation of businesses through changes in processes or organizational design or both.

To date, we haven't been able to pin down the one big reason why Canadian businesses invest less in machinery and technology. It's due partly to a capabilities deficit among our managers, and partly to the lower competitive intensity in Canada that does not force our businesses to invest. The value of the Canadian dollar is not the reason, since we have discovered no relationship in the trend of the dollar's value versus the U.S. dollar and the rate at which we invest in machinery, equipment, and software. While high marginal tax rates on business investment have been a factor in the past, federal and provincial governments' improvements have been making our tax system an advantage for investment. And opening up trade with Europe and China will increase the pressure and support for investment.

Canadians under-invest. This is true for governments that emphasize health care before education, for businesses that do not invest at the same rate as their international counterparts in technology, and for individuals who do not advance their educational attainment as much as they could. Our lower level of economic sophistication is both the cause and the effect of this lower investment profile. Canada needs to retune its economy to a higher level of sophistication.

PART THREE

Recommendations for Achieving Our Prosperity Potential

We've shown how Canada is one of the most competitive and prosperous economies in the world, but we've also shown that it could perform much better if we realized our innovation and productivity potential.

In our review of our strengths and weaknesses, we concluded that Canadians are still not as urbanized as our U.S. counterparts, and this is limiting. We have an advantageous mix of clustered industries – the industries that have the greatest propensity for high productivity and innovation. Unfortunately, we don't compete effectively in many of these industries.

What's holding us back? It's our lack of investment in our own skills and in physical capital like machinery and equipment. Why? It's because our lower level of competitiveness in our industries does not necessitate sophisticated investments. Clearly, we have a circular argument here. But that's exactly our situation – our economy is 'tuned' to a lower level of sophistication, which means we don't need to invest, which in turn keeps us at a lower level of sophistication. And so on. In some sense, we shouldn't fault our businesses or individuals for under-investing. They're not being pushed to invest.

Some would conclude that this is just fine because we are wealthy in global terms. We disagree. We should strive to realize our potential – because our families would benefit from greater economic success. Our governments could help the disadvantaged more and make the investments in our future prosperity.

In the next few chapters, we recommend actions for taking our economy to a higher level of sophistication – that is, an economy with business strategies based on uniqueness, not replication, on skills that are creative, not routine, and on investments that are extensive, not attenuated.

In chapter 7 we review the progress we've made in our tax policy for business investment. In the past, our federal and provincial governments have placed onerous tax burdens on new business investment through high corporate income tax rates, provincial retail sales tax systems, and taxes on capital assets. This problem has now been fixed, and Canada has a better-than-average tax regime for new business investments. But we've simply adopted best tax practices from other countries. Why not become an innovator in tax policy and improve our system even more? Our system of progressive personal income taxation and clawbacks of social programs combines to create very high marginal tax burdens for low-income Canadians trying to improve their economic situation and to contribute more to our overall prosperity. We need creative solutions.

In chapter 8 we review public policy on innovation. Our major challenge federally and provincially is that we are not recognizing that innovation – the profitable development of new products, services, and processes to create value to consumers – is different from invention, which is inventor-driven, not consumer-driven. Invention is obviously important, but the skills needed to innovate and increase productivity are different, and our public policy doesn't recognize this.

In chapter 9 we urge businesses and governments to recognize the importance of management capabilities to our competitiveness and economic success. Strong management drives innovation and productivity and unfortunately Canada has not focused adequately on this important resource.

In chapter 10 we take on the issue of hollowing out. For us and many Canadians, it's a tragedy when a great Canadian firm is taken over by a foreign company. But this phenomenon is not unique to Canada. There isn't much future for large companies that focus only on their domestic markets, especially in smaller countries like ours. Our firms need to bulk up and take on the international competitors in their domestic markets. The good news is that we've grown more of these global leaders in Canada than we've lost.

In chapter 11 we reinforce the importance of international trade in general and set out its specific impact on our innovation performance. Trade provides support for innovation by opening up greater demand for our products and services – and allowing our companies to recoup investments in innovation. Trade also increases the pressure on our firms to enhance their innovation capabilities.

In chapter 12 we examine poverty in Canada, identifying the groups most at risk of being economically challenged. Each of these demographic groups – high school dropouts, single parents, Aboriginal persons, people with disabilities, recent immigrants, and unattached individuals between forty-five and sixty-four – are much more likely to live in poverty. Addressing the specific challenges that each of these groups faces can help them and all Canadians.

To round out our discussion, chapter 13 offers twelve recommendations for making Canada a more productive – and prosperous – country.

7 Tax Smarter for Prosperity

In this chapter, we explore how well our tax system motivates investments by our businesses and work effort by our workers. In both cases, we look at Marginal Effective Tax Rates or METRs. We're pleased about recent changes in federal and provincial tax policies related to business investment and expect that they will help considerably. But these policies have been borrowed from other economies. We'll highlight some innovative approaches to tax reform that we should explore further to help meet our prosperity potential. Some, like the carbon tax, have been debated and dismissed, and we argue that they have merit. Others, like replacing the income tax with a consumption tax, have not been discussed much.

For business investment, the METR measures how much tax is paid on the next, or marginal, dollar of new investment. Types of taxation include corporate income taxes paid annually on the profits from the investment, the sales taxes on the goods purchased for the investment (e.g., construction materials, computers), and annual capital taxes on assets put in place by investments. In other words, how much more must the business earn from this investment to generate an adequate return on the investment?

For workers, we focus on the tax impact on low-income earners of earning the next dollar as they try to move from poverty to a decent income. Here we track the combined effect of the greater income tax low-income workers pay as they increase their earnings, and the benefits they lose because of various program designs.

Lower Business Taxes to Benefit the Average Canadian

We need more investment by our businesses to improve prosperity for the average Canadian. In 2010 Canadian businesses invested $3,800 less per worker – or 36 per cent less – than their competitors in the United States. This matters, because our workers and businesses could create more value if they were supported by the most advanced software and equipment. Our wages are directly related to the amount of value our workers create – through more innovative products or services, or higher efficiency. To gain higher wages and more secure jobs, we need more investment by our businesses.

Do taxes discourage investment? Generally, new business investments increase when taxes on them fall. Our work and that of others have reached the same general conclusion – lowering the cost of business investment means more investment. And this means more innovation and more high-paying jobs. This is because more business investment drives higher wages and more job creation.[1]

Most economists agree that the average Canadian's economic welfare would improve if corporate income tax rates were reduced – accompanied by a revenue-neutral increase in provincial sales tax rate.[2] This is what the Ontario government did in its recent tax reform – cutting corporate rates while extending the provincial sales tax to services (while converting it to a value-added tax).

But the experts are not unanimous. Canadian Auto Workers economist Jim Stanford has recently concluded that business investment depends much more on GDP performance, interest rates, exchange rates, and oil prices than the additional cash flow generated by tax reductions. He states that business tax cuts are 'economically ineffective and distributionally regressive.'[3]

We will follow and contribute to the debate as it proceeds. But it is

Exhibit 31 **Canada is now a low-tax jurisdiction for business investments**

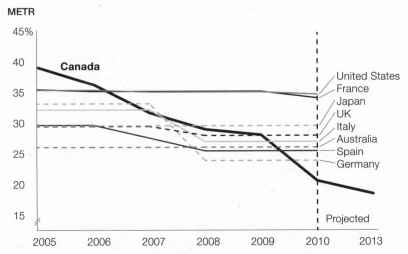

Marginal Effective Tax Rates on capital investment
2005–10

Source: Institute for Competitiveness & Prosperity analysis based on data from Duanjie Chen and Jack Mintz, 'Canada's 2010 Tax Competitiveness Ranking,' SPP Briefing Papers, vol. 4, no. 2, (February 2011); Duanjie Chen and Jack Mintz, 'Federal-Provincial Business Tax Reforms,' SPP Briefing Papers, vol. 4, no. 1, (January 2011); Duanjie Chen and Jack Mintz, 'Business Tax Reform: More Progress Needed – Supplementary Information,' C.D. Howe Institute e-brief, June 2006.

fair to say that, among tax economists, the consensus is that lowering the METR on business investment will improve the economic situation of the average Canadian.

Unfortunately, Canada has traditionally been a high-cost jurisdiction when it comes to taxing new business investment. When we added up all the taxes businesses bear when they invest in new equipment and technology, we found that this rate in Canada has been one of the highest among the world's advanced economies. But, thanks to bold provincial and federal tax policies, Canada is on a path to having lower than average OECD tax rates by 2013 in two ways (Exhibit 31).

First, we have had relatively high tax rates on corporate profits. Businesses make investments to earn profits, so when we tax profits, we in effect tax investments. The federal government has been on track to reducing its corporate income tax rate over the past three years. As well, the federal capital tax was eliminated in 2006 and the provinces have followed suit with a few exceptions for deposit-taking institutions. These changes should encourage businesses to invest.

Second, until Ontario changed its sales tax, businesses paid taxes on their business investments. British Columbia had also changed their sales tax, but unfortunately this was reversed by a provincial referendum in August 2011. The old provincial retail sales taxes applied not just to people buying clothing or appliances; they also applied to businesses when they invested. To be sure, there were many exemptions, since governments had recognized the problem with charging sales taxes on business investments. But still, more than a third of the 'retail' sales tax was paid by businesses making investments or purchasing goods for their operations. By changing their retail sales taxes to value-added taxes, governments have largely eliminated those taxes on business investments and other inputs. When the three Atlantic provinces made this conversion, they saw their business investment in machinery and equipment jump 17 per cent.[4]

The introduction of the harmonized sales tax (HST) in Ontario does not mean that consumers pay more taxes in total. To begin with, reductions in individual income-tax rates accompanied the introduction of the HST in Ontario. There is no tax change at retail for goods that already bore the retail sales tax. In fact, retail prices will actually decline, as the producers of those goods see their costs go down when they stop paying sales taxes on their purchases – and competition forces them to pass on these savings through lower prices. This was the experience in the Atlantic provinces.

To be sure, prices will increase on services that are now being taxed provincially for the first time. But the likely net effect is that the overall average prices for goods and services will increase only slightly.[5] Indeed, in Ontario, prices initially rose only 0.9 per cent following the reform. By December 2010, the effect of tax harmonization had fallen to a 0.6 per cent increase, as businesses passed on their tax savings to consumers in the form of lower prices.[6] British Columbia had a similar result: prices rose only 0.6 per cent as a result of its reform before the tax change was reversed.[7]

It is fair to say that converting retail sales taxes on goods to value-added taxes on goods and services affects those with lower incomes more than others. But the Ontario and British Columbia governments exempted items like books and children's clothing from the new tax. And they introduced tax credits for those with lower income to help alleviate the tax burden on services. For many families, these measures compensate for the higher sales tax.

Taken together, these tax improvements move Canada from being well above the OECD average in tax rates for new business investment to being better than average. As a result, by one estimate, Ontario's capital investment will increase by $47 billion by 2020, creating 591,000 new jobs and $29 billion in labour and investment income.[8] In British Columbia, the new tax policies put in place in 2010 would have generated $14 billion in capital investment and 141,000 new jobs.[9]

We've made great progress in Canada in addressing high marginal tax rates on new business investments and this will help the average Canadian. The necessary changes were relatively easy to identify; we now turn to a different challenge where the problem is equally obvious, but solutions are elusive.

Lower METRs for Low-Income Workers

Sandra Schmidt is trying to move up the income ladder. As a single mother without reliable child care, she is unable to take on a regular 9-to-5 job. And her lack of a post- secondary degree reduces her opportunities to work in high-paying jobs. But she has been able to stitch together some part-time work – doing some data-entry work at her dad's bank and working weekends at the local Tim Hortons. She really chases the hours during summer months when her mother has more time to babysit. In her 'spare time,' Sandra is completing her university credits.

Last year Sandra's T4s added up to $15,000, a 50 per cent increase from what she earned the previous year. But she didn't feel as if she had made great strides. At $15,000, Sandra still avoids provincial and federal income taxes. But she lost three-quarters of her Ontario Works benefits, which fell from $6,343 at $10,000 income to $3,577 at $15,000 – and while she saw it as a psychological step forward to be less reliant on welfare, it was definitely a financial step backward.

In addition, her Working Income Tax Benefit (WITB), a federal tax credit for low-income workers, fell from $1,497 to $917. Across several other programs for low-income Canadians living in Ontario – the Canada Child Tax Benefit, the Ontario Child Benefit, the Ontario Child Care Supplement for Working Families, and GST/HST and property-tax credits – Sandra lost benefits worth $140. So, while her gross earnings increased by $5,000, her take-home pay increased by $2,046. In other words, she lost about sixty cents per dollar of increased wages, a METR of 60 per cent. While we are all rooting for Sandra to keep working and get on the path to income mobility, our benefits system discourages people like her from working more.

What's going on here? Why do we make it so hard for people to break out of poverty and get ahead?

These high marginal rates are largely the product of clawbacks of tax credits, benefits, and transfer programs rather than statutory personal income tax rates. People like Sandra earning less than $20,000 still do not pay income taxes. Instead, by designing our social programs to be means-tested – benefits are phased out at certain income thresholds – we claw back benefits and in effect impose a 'tax' on new income as these thresholds are crossed.

Overall, lower-income Canadians continue to face high marginal tax rates as they attempt to improve their economic circumstances. As an example, for every new dollar earned by a single earner on welfare, fifty cents of the welfare benefit will be reduced. This clawback feature is present in all social benefits. Adding in the progressivity of income tax, our tax and welfare system can result in exceedingly high METRs. A single earner in Ontario in 2009 with annual earnings around $15,000 lost fifty-four cents of every dollar of increased earnings through benefit clawbacks and tax increases. In addition, our welfare and taxation polices result in low-income earners losing in-kind benefits like social housing and health and dental services as they gain income through work.

This is a difficult problem to fix, since it is the result of two fundamentals in our tax and social-benefit policies: benefits should accrue to those with lower, not higher, incomes; and our income-tax system should be progressive. What is clear, however, is that each program needs to be assessed with respect to its impact on marginal effective tax rates of low-income earners when combined with all other programs.

Some design improvements in the WITB could alleviate high METRs for low-income workers. This benefit is designed to supplement low earnings for people trying to move out of welfare through employment. While benefits are fairly small currently, the WITB, with more funding, represents a significant opportunity to help low-income earners break out of poverty. But it needs to be redesigned to encourage full-time, rather than part-time, work. It currently reaches its maximum benefit around fourteen hours of work weekly for a single earner. It should be changed to reach its maximum around thirty-two hours – closer to full-time employment.

Thus, while benefit programs provide valuable assistance to low-income families, an unintended consequence of benefit clawbacks is that families progressing toward higher income levels can face a dramatically higher marginal tax rate on their additional income. Further, the rates are high because the clawbacks typically sit on top of each other. Thus, over certain income ranges, effective tax rates are punishingly high. On average, low-income earners in Canada have zero tax rates. But, at the margin, effective tax rates can be quite high. Average tax rates (net of benefits) are progressive and are still below zero for families with a taxable income below $40,000. Nevertheless, the persistently high marginal effective rates on taxable income do not encourage more workforce participation and work effort. The potential negative impact of high METRs caused by clawbacks is high for single-parent families, like Sandra's.[10]

Any progressive tax and benefit system will have the feature of high marginal tax burdens at certain points of the income scale. The problem in Canada is that our system for low-income earners is characterized by plateaus, not by spikes. Sandra's brother Kevin earns $75,000 in his job. In 2009, his income exceeded $72,000 and he moved from a marginal tax rate of 31 per cent[11] to a higher tax bracket of 33 per cent as well as a higher charge for Ontario's health premium. As his income increased from $72,000 to $72,500, his take-home pay on the extra $500 was only $219 – hence his marginal effective tax paid was $281 or 56.2 per cent. But, beyond that hurdle, the health-premium increase had been paid and was not affected by more income. So his marginal tax rate settled at 33 per cent – until the next spike over $200,000. But for low-income earners – whether they are unattached individuals or single parents like Sandra – the METR stays high for a broader income range (Exhibit 32).

The challenge in designing tax and benefit systems is to balance the need to support lower-income individuals and families and the need to ensure that incentives to work and upgrade skills are preserved. In many instances, it might be that higher earnings that move individuals into higher brackets – or cause low-income assistance to disappear at a higher rate – eliminate or significantly reduce the incentive for an individual to make an effort to increase his or her economic well-being through additional work effort or skill upgrades.

Equity demands that taxes are borne by those most able to pay them. Clearly, the current system is placing the highest marginal rates on lower-income Canadians. We see several smart ways to redress this imbalance.

Smooth out METRs

The federal and provincial governments can improve incentives to work through a closer integration of our tax and transfer systems to smooth out the high marginal tax rates created by the current clawback system. Since this involves large portions of our social programs and tax policy at the federal and provincial levels, reform would be com-

Exhibit 32 · **Marginal Effective Tax Rates are very high for a low-income single earner**

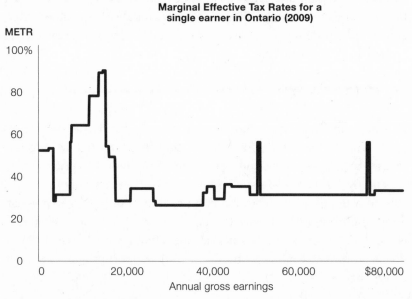

Marginal Effective Tax Rates for a single earner in Ontario (2009)

Note: Assume single earner with no children.
Source: Institute for Competitiveness & Prosperity analysis based on data from Don Drummond and Gillian Manning, *From Welfare to Work in Ontario: Still the Road Less Travelled*, TD Economics Special Report, 2005; John Stapleton, Open Policy Ontario.

plicated and time-consuming. We recognize that changes at specific income thresholds or in the design of various programs in one area can have unintended negative effects elsewhere.

At this time of fiscal restraint, governments are not receptive to recommendations that add to their spending – and fixing the high METR problem for low-income Canadians will likely cost more. But we think it is a journey worth embarking on. If we can get this right, the added spending will help reduce poverty and increase the contribution to our prosperity by those who are currently marginalized. Reform requires cooperation between the federal and provincial governments to redesign tax credits, such as the Child Tax Credit. Currently, the two levels of government are shifting toward more personal deductions rather than income-tested child-care benefits; the Universal Child Care Benefit is an example. This move will help reduce high METRs for low-income earners moving up the earnings ladder. Other options include lowering taxes for all families with children and reducing the threshold at which benefit reductions begin while decreasing the dollar value of benefits as real incomes grow over time.

Provide Direct Assistance to Lower-Income Workers

In some circumstances, traditional income-support measures such as tax credits and other government transfers may not be effective in assisting low-income individuals and families. In certain cases, expanding fundamental assistance programs,[12] such as labour-market skills development, skills-upgrading programs, and job-search assistance, might be a better way to help individuals adjust to economic change and increase the economic opportunities available to them. This would reduce reliance on income from support programs that are clawed back.

Allow Higher Private-Income Exemptions for Seniors

Our low-income seniors face marginal rates exceeding 50 per cent at earnings between $10,000 and $20,000. This occurs largely because of the stiff clawback rates to the Guaranteed Income Supplement.[13] Possible reform options include permitting a private-income exemption before the income testing of benefits begins. This would allow seniors' employment income to accrue toward a partial exemption from income testing or a reduction in clawback rates.[14]

Reduce the Basic Personal Allowance and Marginal Rates

The federal and provincial governments could consider sharply reducing the Basic Personal Allowance (BPA) and supporting low-income earners more directly with enhanced income support or other initiatives.

Any income below the BPA, $10,822 in 2012, is exempt from federal income tax. The problem with the BPA is that most of this benefit goes to people who are not low-income earners. Consequently, marginal tax rates are higher than they need to be, since governments must replace the tax revenue lost by the BPA. A better approach would be to lower – or scrap – the BPA, find more efficient ways to help low-income earners, and reduce marginal tax rates on all other taxpayers. The benefit of lowering the BPA and marginal tax rates is that income earners would face lower tax rates on the last dollar they earned rather than the first.

Assess Other Tax Innovations

We are very supportive of the current improvements in tax policy across Canada. But these changes, as we've noted, simply adopt best practices from around the world. We have not had an innovative tax policy since indexing personal income tax brackets in 1974. The federal and provincial governments should consider real innovation in our tax system.

Implement Cash-Flow Accounting for Investments

In its March 2011 budget, the federal government proposed a two-year extension of the temporary accelerated capital-cost allowance rate for machinery and equipment investments made in the manufacturing and processing sector. In its 2011 federal election platform, the New Democratic Party proposed a four-year extension.

Accelerating the capital-cost allowance rate means that businesses can write off the cost of new investments against income more quickly, thereby reducing current income taxes. Traditionally, when businesses invest in assets that are in place for longer than a year, they can deduct the costs of this investment over the life of the asset – thereby matching costs and benefits. Typical annual capital-cost allowance rates, depending on the assets, range between 4 per cent for buildings and around 50 per cent for computer equipment and software.

The temporary accelerated rate for machinery and equipment in the manufacturing and processing sector is 50 per cent (versus the traditional 30 per cent), meaning that businesses see tax reductions early in the life of these assets, but these reductions are recaptured in later years when businesses have no deductions left. In effect, through the time value of money, businesses face lower investment costs with an accelerated capital-cost allowance. The expectation is that businesses will make more investments, thereby creating jobs and improving our productivity. Governments often turn to this measure when they are trying to stimulate growth.

Why not make the accelerated capital-cost allowance permanent for all businesses? And why not go to a one-year write-off? In essence, businesses would operate on a cash-flow basis for tax purposes. In the year when they make a major investment, their tax liability is reduced. This approach would entail a very modest cost for government. Admittedly, it would produce just a small increase in capital investment and GDP – but the net effect will be positive, including the benefits of a much simpler corporate-tax regime.

Eliminate Corporate Income Taxes

A more dramatic and effective approach would be to eliminate corporate taxes altogether. Corporations are accounting and legal entities – they are not people. And people, not corporations, pay taxes.

Some might argue that eliminating corporate taxes would be a boon to the wealthy. But, if the goal is to have a progressive tax system, then the most effective way to realize progressivity is through the marginal rate structure in the personal income tax. To the extent that corporate-tax elimination increases dividend payments – and this advantages higher-income earners more than pension funds – the personal rate structure could be modified.

This is a simple idea but with many 'knock-on' effects. We urge the federal government to explore the idea in more detail because of the potential benefit it has for our innovation, productivity, and prosperity.

Tax Consumption, not Income or Investment

Governments should focus more on taxing consumption, not savings and investment. They should increase the federal and provincial goods and services taxes and reduce taxes on income and investment. Governments should also consider shifting the personal income tax to a personal consumption tax. Under such a tax, people would report not only their income but their annual savings. The difference is consumption, and that could be the basis for personal taxation.[15] Tax rates would maintain their progressivity, so that those who consume more (in most cases, equivalent to those with higher income) would pay higher tax rates. But the tax system would motivate investment over consumption more fully.

The idea is not as radical as one might think, for recent income-tax changes are already taking us in this direction. Increased Registered Retirement Savings Plan (RRSP) limits mean that more income can be tax-deferred by investing it, and the Tax Free Saving Account does not avoid taxes on the investment but shelters the return on the investment from income taxes.

Consider a Carbon Tax

To address environmental and energy concerns, many governments here in Canada and around the world are putting in place energy-pricing regimes that encourage the rapid deployment of renewable-energy generation. A favourite saying among tax experts is that, if you want more of something in society, tax it less; if you want less, tax it more. This aphorism applies to the environment, energy security, and green jobs. If we want to make progress on these fronts, we should seriously consider taxing carbon emissions – even though political support for this is very low right now.

A typical element of current approaches to environmental policy is a guaranteed feed-in-tariff (FIT) – a commitment by the public energy authority to pay much higher than prevailing market rates for energy created by favoured sources. Because the economics of sources like solar and wind have not yet delivered energy at a competitive cost, FIT proponents argue that these temporary subsidies are necessary to bring generating capacity on line and to stimulate the process of reducing costs as experience is gained. But there are few examples of such subsidies getting costs down and then being eliminated. In addition, many FIT schedules advantage specific technologies like wind and solar. But it is not clear that these technologies will turn out to be the best solutions for addressing carbon emissions cost-effectively. In the end, ratepayers may be paying a higher cost for electricity without a commensurate benefit in emissions reductions.[16] There's a billboard in rural Ontario that announces, 'Turbines go up and bills go up.'

FITs price one input: electricity from renewable sources. But they do not deliver the outcome we want: reductions in greenhouse gas (GHG) emissions. To reduce GHG emissions and promote innovation across Canada, we continue to recommend that the federal and provincial governments consider a carbon tax instead. A carbon tax would, like a FIT, impose costs on households and businesses, but since it remains agnostic regarding technologies and prices GHG emissions directly, it is likely to achieve greater emissions reductions at lower cost. The revenues generated from a carbon tax could be used to lower personal or corporate income taxes. As both an environmental and an economic policy, a carbon tax is the better option.

An alternative market-based approach would be a cap-and-trade system. This has the advantage of setting a desired level of carbon emissions – the cap – and then allowing firms to trade permits to produce carbon emissions. In a carbon-tax environment, there is no guarantee that the chosen tax rate will reduce emissions to the desired level. However, over time, the tax rate can be moved to respond to emission results. A cap-and-trade system has significant implementation challenges. For example, it would be difficult to establish initial allowances and governments would have to deal with arguments for special treatment by various industries. On balance, we prefer the carbon tax, because it has the advantage of being much simpler to implement than cap-and-trade.

The past few years have seen an improvement in our federal and provincial tax policies. Lowering taxes on business investment is not just favourable for businesses; it is favourable for individuals. The governments of Ontario and British Columbia took important initiatives when the easier political strategy would have been to wait until economic conditions were better. Many argue that governments cannot 'take bold action' and 'do the right thing,' because that's not politically feasible. The British Columbia referendum helps that argument. But the Ontario government, which implemented the new tax policy, showed that it is possible to do both. All governments should consider an additional set of improvements and innovations in tax policy.

8 Make Public Policy on Innovation More Innovative

Public policy to increase innovation is not working. A major part of the problem is that our governments have developed policies to drive invention, not innovation. The two are not the same, and we must recognize this to achieve effective public policy. We also need to pursue true innovation in our public policy for innovation.

How Do Invention and Innovation Differ?

Invention can be defined as the creation or discovery of something new to the world. Inventions are often producer-driven, following an inventor's curiosity or area of expertise. While they are new, inventions in scientific institutes or corporate labs may or may not have any use in the world.

Innovation is customer-driven, providing a new product or process that adds value to somebody's life. Innovations can improve economic, health, or social well-being (Exhibit 33).

Innovations are often built from inventions. Mobile telephony required new findings in cellular technology, and the Internet became widespread after the invention of fibre-optic technology. But we should not just assume that inventions naturally lead to innovation. And even if they do, that often takes a long time. The U.S. National Research Council found that, in the communications and computer-technologies

Exhibit 33 **Invention and innovation: What's the difference?**

INVENTION	INNOVATION
A new-to-the-world discovery/creation	A product, service, or process that creates new value for customers
Driven primarily by inventor curiosity or research interest	Driven primarily by desire to add customer value
Merit defined by uniqueness	Merit defined by profitable deployment
Based primarily on scientific skills	Based on a broad set of strategic, marketing, operational, and technical skills

Source: Institute for Competitiveness & Prosperity.

sector, the average time from invention to market was more than twenty years. As scientist and designer William Buxton puts it, 'innovation is far more about prospecting, mining, refining, and adding value to gold than it is about alchemy.'[1]

Innovation creates value in several ways:

- it can make it possible for consumers to do something that they could not have done at all or as well before; or
- it can reduce the cost of doing what consumers were previously doing – in two ways:
  - delivering the same benefits as existing offerings, but at a lower price; or
  - maintaining the price of the product or service but reducing overall costs of use.

Canada's global leaders provide examples of these sources of innovation.

Innovation Enhances the Consumer Experience

Four Seasons, the world's leading luxury-hotel chain, has succeeded by offering a different guest-service model than its competitors. From its consumer research, it concluded that luxury for guests meant not grand architecture and décor, the prevailing approach in the business, but rather service that made guests feel that they were special. Acting on that insight, Four Seasons achieved the highest guest ratings and the best customer loyalty in the industry.

In a similar way, Cirque du Soleil, the world's leading circus, recognized that traditional circus acts did not fulfill consumers' desires for exciting entertainment. It reinvented the whole concept of a 'circus' and appealed to a wider and more affluent audience.

Innovation Reduces Costs and Consumer Prices

Harlequin, the world's largest publisher of romance fiction, realized that if each of its books had exactly the same number of pages and that this number equalled one sheet on the printing press, it could print its books at a lower cost than its competitors. The books could also be shipped in identical cube-efficient boxes and be more easily displayed on uniform retailers' shelves. Harlequin also developed mail-order book clubs for its most loyal readers, lowering distribution costs and eliminating the hassle of going to bookstores.

McCain is the leading producer and seller of frozen-potato products in many parts of the world. Most of us would likely expect that its main business is branded consumer products. But it's not. Its biggest business by far is selling frozen french fries to restaurants and other food-service organizations. Food-service operators save considerable labour costs because they no longer have to peel, cut, and fry potatoes from scratch.

Manulife, one of the world's five largest life insurance companies, provides another example of innovation to reduce customer costs. It assembled the technology and developed business processes to create the Manulife One account, enabling homeowners to optimize their use of any excess cash to pay down their mortgage or to pay off their credit-card debt, thus allowing significant savings on interest costs. In addition, it used its experience with individual and group RRSPs in Canada to become a leader in more consumer-friendly retirement-savings products across the globe.

Does Our Innovation Policy Support Invention or Innovation?

Federal and provincial innovation policies have done little to fuel the consumer-driven innovations that made these companies global leaders. Current public policy assumes that, if a scientist working in a laboratory or an R&D department comes up with something new, that is innovation. And anything else is not. But that is invention – which should not be confused with innovation.

Obviously, invention is important. But little that our governments do in their current innovation policies helps inventors better understand consumers. Without deep understanding of consumers or without the pressure of a competitor trying to win them away, it is very unlikely that an inventor will be an innovator. Unless policy changes, we will continue to spend billions of dollars funding invention and get little innovation to show for it.

Of course, there are notable examples of success in our governments' innovation policy. R&D support helped Nortel create the world's first Class 5 fully digital network-communications switch, the DMS 100. This was an example of consumer-driven innovation. Existing analog switches were not up to the task of carrying growing telephone traffic speedily and reliably; carriers needed something better. Nortel sales and marketing people saw this opportunity and collaborated with their research colleagues at Bell-Northern Research to produce the digital innovation. Even though AT&T Network Systems (later Lucent Technologies) dominated the U.S. telecommunications market at the time, Nortel was more customer-focused and won.

Certainly, too, R&D support helped Research In Motion to invent and improve the BlackBerry, Canada's most important technology product. But the BlackBerry success story has much to do with innovative distribution agreements with telecommunications carriers.

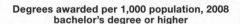

Exhibit 34 **Canada produces fewer business graduates than the United States**

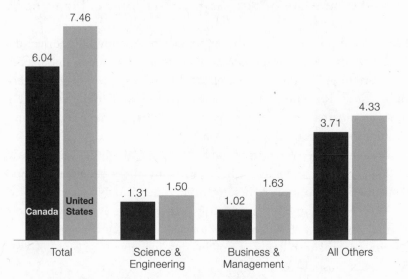

Degrees awarded per 1,000 population, 2008
bachelor's degree or higher

| Total | Science & Engineering | Business & Management | All Others |

Note: Calendar year 2008 for Canada. Academic year 2007–8 for United States.
Source: Institute for Competitiveness & Prosperity, Association of Universities & Colleges of Canada; U.S. Department of Education, National Center for Education Statistics.

Our public innovation policy emphasizes the hard sciences and does not adequately recognize the importance of business and management processes for innovation. Our competitiveness and prosperity are built on a solid base of excellence in the sciences. And leading high-technology firms are founded by science and engineering graduates. But successful innovation requires a balance of skills from the hard sciences as well as the humanities and social sciences, such as problem solving and communication skills. These other skills are important to achieve a successful transition from start-up to thriving businesses.

The flawed premise leads to an *imbalance in our focus* on scientific and engineering skills over social science and humanities research, especially business education. As we have seen, Canada produces fewer

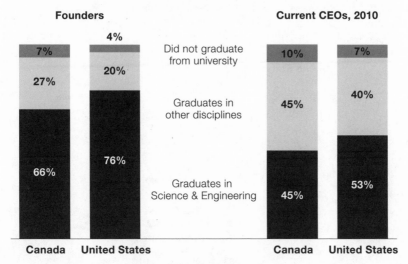

Exhibit 35 **Science skills are important for founders,
but other skills matter for mature firms**

Education disciplines of large high-tech firms'
founders and current CEOs

Founders   Current CEOs, 2010

Did not graduate
from university

Graduates in
other disciplines

Graduates in
Science & Engineering

Canada   United States   Canada   United States

Leading high technology firms

Source: Institute for Competitiveness & Prosperity based on companies' public data. Canadian companies are
ten high-tech global leaders (fifteen founders, eleven current CEOs). U.S. companies are thirty *Fortune 1,000*
high-tech companies less than thirty years old (fifty-one founders, thirty current CEOs).

university degrees than the United States – about 19 per cent fewer
degrees per capita overall. In the science and engineering discipline,
the gap is only 13 per cent while in business and management it is 37
per cent. The gap in all other disciplines is 14 per cent (Exhibit 34).

In the real world of high-tech innovative firms, we do not see a pre-
ponderance of science skills at the top. Many of the leading high-tech
firms were founded by science and engineering graduates. But, as the
firms developed, formal business skills became much more important
(Exhibit 35).

We will not progress on innovation in Canada until our policies
target innovation broadly rather than focus narrowly on invention. It
is important to support a higher-education system, where curiosity-

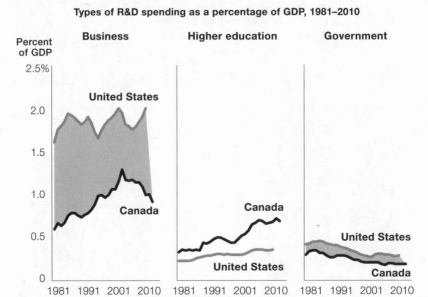

Exhibit 36 **Canada invests significantly in public R&D but not business R&D**

Types of R&D spending as a percentage of GDP, 1981–2010

Note: U.S. results available only to 2009.
Source: Institute for Competitiveness & Prosperity analysis based on data from Statistics Canada (Table 358–0001); U.S. National Science Foundation (Division of Science Resources Statistics, *National Patterns of R&D Resources: 2008 Data Update, NSF 07–331*).

based research is funded. But we should not assume that much of this will lead to innovation. Inventions searching for a use have never been a high-payoff endeavour.

Our governments should also recognize that investing in publicly funded R&D, especially through universities, has not produced significant innovation and productivity growth. Canada invests much more in public R&D than most other advanced economies. But our businesses invest much less in R&D (Exhibit 36) and, as we have seen, in technology than their U.S. counterparts.

Let's Be Innovative in Our Innovation Policy

Successful innovation actually means trying things that are unproven

– optimally, that have never been tried before. The innovation examples from our global leaders that we referred to earlier in this chapter were untried and unproven. As we look back on Steve Jobs's incredible career, we see that Apple's biggest successes derived from doing positively unproven things – like controlling a PC with a mouse, twinning the iPod with iTunes, linking the iPhone with the App Store, and creating the tablet. Apple couldn't analyze and benchmark the success of somebody else who had done these things already to demonstrate that its ideas would succeed. The company had no way of knowing that it was going to have absolute smash hits on its hands. That is what is required for innovation; otherwise, we would call it something else – perhaps replication.

Canadian innovation policy pretty much follows what is done elsewhere, and does it here. If other jurisdictions have research-granting councils, then we do too. If others have Centres of Excellence, then we decide to have some of those too. If Israel has a chief scientist, we get one of those too.

Let's remember that some of the most effective policy moves Canada has ever made were unique – they were actually innovative, like indexing tax brackets to combat bracket creep and setting strict inflation targets to guide monetary policy. We didn't just replicate; others were left to do that, while we prospered through policy innovation.

We could explore new ways to connect inventors who care about innovation with business people who want to turn inventions into innovations that will excite consumers. Perhaps through business and engineering schools, we could develop programs to team up inventors and innovators. These programs would be more than course work; instead, they would match up people to create real innovations and involve innovation financiers. Public funding could be available for winning innovations. A good example to follow would be the Natural Sciences and Engineering Research Council (NSERC), which is helping to connect scientists and business people with programs that encourage Canadian companies to participate and invest in post-secondary research projects.

We Can Teach Innovation in Primary and Secondary School

But let's start even earlier. Think about how very little of K-12 education currently is at all about innovation. That has never been its focus. Its focus is about teaching our young people what is, not what could be. Arguably, that was fully appropriate for a given place and time, but, just as arguably, it is no longer a sensible mix for this place and this time.

So let's do something unique that is in keeping with a century that is going to be more about innovation than we have ever seen. With global competition and low-cost jurisdictions like China, India, and Brazil advancing more quickly than ever before, we need to be an innovation nation. Let's become the first nation on the planet to have universal education in innovation by explicitly and clearly teaching innovation in the primary and secondary school system.

One of the biggest problems with the notion of teaching innovation is the widespread superstition that innovation is some kind of God-given capability. Either an organization has it or not; either a person was born with it or not. Nothing could be further from the truth: innovation can be taught. Of course, like all things in life, you can take a horse to water but can't make it drink. A person or organization needs to want to learn innovation; but if they do, they can upgrade their capabilities from whatever level they started from.

In 2000 A.G. Lafley became chief executive officer of Procter & Gamble (P&G), the biggest consumer-packaged-goods company in the world and a legendary innovator. At the time, the company's innovation output was lagging. Its success rate on innovation projects was below industry benchmarks, and its competitors were catching up. Lafley knew that he had to improve the company's innovation capability for its long-term competitive future. He and his vice-president of design strategy and innovation, Claudia Kotchka, called on leaders from Stanford University (David Kelley), the Institute of Design at the Illinois Institute of Technology (Patrick Whitney), and the Rotman School of Management (Roger Martin) to help P&G grow its innovative capability.

The team created an executive training experience called Design-Works that was soon rolled out to the whole of P&G worldwide. Many things contributed to the innovation renaissance at P&G, which resulted in it winning the Edison Award as the top American innovation company of the decade. But DesignWorks was most certainly one of them.

After the successful installation of DesignWorks at P&G, Martin brought the methodology back to the Rotman School of Management where, led by DesignWorks Director Heather Fraser, it was taught both to MBA students and to large corporations, including General Electric, Medtronic, Nestle, and Pfizer. It taught participants approaches to understanding customers in a deep and holistic way; to visualize and develop prototypes for serving them; and to create business systems that build competitive advantage based on these innovations.

The success with some of the world's finest corporations has confirmed that the art and process of innovation can be taught. The always innovative government of Singapore engaged Rotman to open Design-Works Singapore to work with its high-potential medium-sized businesses to enhance and accelerate their global competitiveness through innovation. But Singapore enabled Rotman DesignWorks to test its innovation pedagogy with an even more important audience: secondary school students, the future of its economy. This experience literally half-way around the world enabled Rotman DesignWorks to launch a pilot program in Ontario secondary schools. This is innovation built in Canada, tested with global corporations and students across the globe, and applied initially with tremendous success in our country.

Innovation could be taught to all secondary school students in Canada to create an innovation nation unlike any other on the planet. That would be innovation in innovation policy. With such initiatives, public policy will help us create a vibrant twenty-first-century economy.

Innovation Needs Venture Capital and Venture Capital Needs Innovation

Another element of public policy related to innovation is supporting the supply of venture capital. Venture capital is very important to helping innovative companies develop. The term refers to investments made in start-up companies typically pioneering new technologies that require significant cash to develop them for market readiness. The investors have secured access to pools of funds and usually have specialized knowledge of the technology or its potential markets. Venture capital is risky and most investments fail. But if enough of the venture-capital investments are hugely successful, like Google, Apple, and Genentech, the net returns can be huge.

Young innovative companies have benefited significantly from venture-capital investments. In Canada, the generally accepted view has been that we have inadequate venture-capital funds available for our up-and-coming companies. A major element of federal and provincial policy has been to encourage the average Canadian to invest in venture capital through attractive tax benefits. But the assumption that we need to emphasize the quantity of capital available over the quality has meant we have created an industry in Canada that earns terrible returns (Exhibit 37). The most important policy tool has been the labour-sponsored investment funds – a favourable tax treatment for small investors.

A few years ago, the Schmidts' investment adviser convinced Michael and Maria to put part of their annual RRSP contribution into a labour-sponsored investment fund (LSIF). He pointed out quite rightly that the tax breaks would be so good that great investment returns weren't critical. But Michael and Maria, as smart as they are, are not the investors we want in venture capital.

Venture capital needs sophisticated investors who can actually provide industry expertise and management guidance to the start-up companies they're investing in. These investors need to be patient and have a tolerance for risk. But the LSIFs attracted the Schmidts and other small 'retail' investors who bought the funds as part of their RRSP. Their poor design has been a major contributor to the poor performance of Canada's venture-capital industry. On a positive note, Ontario is phasing out the special tax treatment for these funds; less positively,

Exhibit 37   **Recent returns on venture capital have been abysmal in Canada and the United States**

Three-year venture capital annualized returns

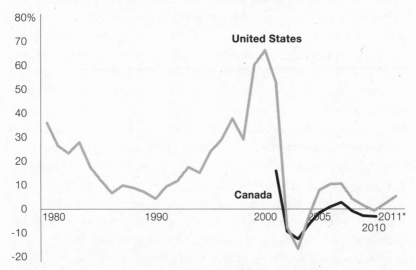

* U.S. results through 30 June, 2011. 2011 results not available for Canada.
Note: Canadian venture-capital performance data are available only from 2001 onward.
Source: Institute for Competitiveness & Prosperity analysis based on data from Canada's Venture Capital & Private Equity Association (CVCA); U.S. National Venture Capital Association (NVCA); Thomson Reuters; and Cambridge Associates LLC.

some provinces are considering introducing special tax treatment for LSIFs.

But setting aside the poor design of labour-sponsored funds, are there alternatives to the traditional venture-capital model? The amount of available funds in the venture-capital industry has shrunk considerably. But this is not unique to Canada. Available venture-capital funds are now also at a much lower level in the United States – declining by more than a third from 2007 to 2010. And the returns in the U.S. market aren't exactly stellar.

At a time when available venture capital is much less plentiful, traditional approaches aimed at creating large pools of funds with significant investments per company may not be appropriate. Moreover,

Canada's venture-capital industry invests far fewer dollars per company than its U.S. equivalent.

There may be an opportunity to turn our subscale investments into an advantage. Observers of the industry have noted that venture capital has become too capital-intensive and has lost its traditional position as a 'no-frills' funder of start-ups. Eric Ries, entrepreneur and consultant to the venture-capital industry, coined the term 'lean start-ups' and, along with Stanford professor Steve Blank, developed a new approach to venture capital. Based on elements of design thinking – iteration, fact-based decision making, and experimentation – lean start-up organizations are temporary in nature, designed to discover and implement a profitable business model that can start small and be scaled up quickly for commercial success.[2]

At its core, the lean start-up minimizes the amount of cash required in the early stages of a company. Lean start-up managers are challenged to earn revenue from day one and make investments only as revenue is generated. This requires real customers from the outset, as well as continuous interaction with them to guide iterative product development. According to Blank and Ries, the lean start-up has a low burn rate of its cash by design, not by crisis.

Lean start-ups place a premium on management agility to test hypotheses and answer unknowns. As Ries observes, 'the agile practices have to be adapted, shifting the focus somewhat from generating stuff to learning about what customers will want. Most technology start-ups fail not because the technology doesn't work, but because they are making something that there is not a real market for.'[3]

Product development is carried out in a continuous cycle measured in hours, not years, and is necessarily coupled with customer contact. Costs are minimized through the relentless search for supporting open-source programming tools and easily distributed web-based software. Examples of successful lean start-ups include Dropbox, a file-sharing and synchronization service, which started in 2007 with $1.2 million in seed funding, gathered another $6 million a year later, and reached the four-million-customer milestone in 2010; and Grockit, an online educational network to help students of all ages improve academic results, which started with first-round funding of $2.5 million and has since raised $15 million.

Lean start-ups are a promising antidote to the current ills of Canadian and American venture-capital business models. Given the challenges of achieving large investments in start-up companies, it would be wise for Canadian industries and governments to understand this concept more deeply. Our business schools and incubating organizations like MaRS in Toronto may be able to establish formal courses in lean start-up ventures, similar to the popular 'Evaluating Entrepreneurial Opportunities,' a practical course offered at Stanford's Graduate School of Business. Opportunities may exist for small investments by provincial and federal governments to help the lean-start-up approach gain traction in Canada.

As we have seen, our prosperity gap is a productivity gap; and our productivity gap is an innovation gap. Despite extensive funding of innovation agendas across Canada over the years, we aren't making progress. Until we adopt a more sensible way to think about structures for innovation and to become truly innovative in our innovation polices, we will continue to lag other countries.

9 Strengthen Management Talent

In the previous chapter, we discussed briefly the over-emphasis of our innovation policies on hard-science skills. We agree that these are critical for Canada's innovation success. But Canada has not devoted adequate attention to developing our management strength – a critical complement to science and engineering talent.

As we have seen, our senior and middle managers do not have fundamentally different attitudes toward competition, risk taking, and innovation from their U.S. counterparts. Nor do they have a different culture or outlook. Instead, our lagging innovation and productivity are driven by underdeveloped management capabilities – lower educational attainment and less diffusion of best-management practices; and context – less competitive intensity in the markets and the lack of sophisticated customers. Consistent with the findings from Deloitte Canada which we discussed earlier, these factors mean that it is easier to 'get by' in Canada with complacency in our management cadre.

Management talent is important for innovation and prosperity, and the adoption of the best management techniques is correlated with higher productivity gains. Management capabilities in our manufacturing and retail sectors offer examples of the current state of management in Canada.

Management Talent Is Important in the Innovation System

Innovation is the result of the ongoing interaction of two elements in an Innovation System – support and pressure. Both are critical for success and need to work in balance. *Support* for innovation includes the activities and resources dedicated to increasing the stock of innovation, including highly qualified personnel and their facilities and resources. Support for innovation comes from capable managers who understand the importance of innovation activities and pursue strategies based on innovative products and processes. *Pressure* for innovation comes from the combination of customer insistence on new products and process breakthroughs and competitive rivalry. This combination makes complacency untenable.

Strong management is important in both elements of the Innovation System. The management function includes goal setting, organization building, resource allocation, and results monitoring. It also includes actions in enterprise finance, sales and promotion, production and delivery, and people development.

Strong management is a significant driver of support in an effective Innovation System. Capable managers support the demand for innovation through a keen understanding of the need for product and process innovation in developing company capabilities. Senior management drives the resource allocation in a company and thus stimulates the demand for innovation. Management skills are critical to organizing R&D efforts, setting priorities, developing strategies, and acquiring resources. Financiers of innovation require both solid scientific knowledge and management skills. Strategic capabilities provide critical support to high-quality financing decisions.

Strong management also provides the necessary pressure that fuels the demand for innovation. As customers, good managers drive the requirement for innovation by suppliers; this, in turn, drives overall demand for innovation. Good managers also pressure industry rivals to be innovative in order to succeed – in fact, to survive.

Hence, in building an innovative firm or an innovative economy, management talent matters. Senior management in the firms we discussed in the previous chapter were the drivers and implementers of their innovation.

We also saw that, as successful high-technology firms in Canada matured, the importance of technical skills at the top of the organization was matched by the importance of other skills, including management capability. And our economy does value higher skills in analytical and social-intelligence capabilities that lead innovation and upgrading.

Canada Lacks Sufficient Sophisticated Management Talent

An important opportunity for improving Canada's innovation and productivity performance lies in strengthening the management talent in our economy. Our managers generally have significantly less education than their U.S. counterparts. Only 35 per cent of our managers possess a university degree versus 53 per cent of U.S. managers (Exhibit 38).

If the link between education and innovation can be drawn, it is apparent why we are not demanding more innovation in Canada. The more educated managers are, the more likely it is that they will have been exposed to the latest advances in management techniques and technology. The lower education level of our human-capital resources means that we are less able to compete in a technology-based knowledge economy and to serve sophisticated and demanding customers in the global marketplace. At the pinnacle of Canadian corporations, we find a lower incidence of MBAs than in the United States.[1]

Innovative firms report disadvantages in management as a key constraint. One of the most significant challenges they face in their development is gaining access to 'managerial talent to hire.' Importantly, this challenge is perceived to be a significant disadvantage for them against their most important competitors, who tend to be in the United States (Exhibit 39).

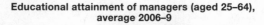

Exhibit 38 **Canadian managers are less well educated than
their U.S. counterparts**

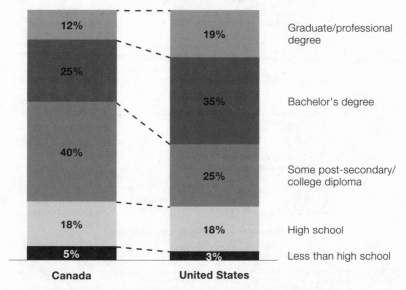

**Educational attainment of managers (aged 25–64),
average 2006–9**

Canada	United States	
12%	19%	Graduate/professional degree
25%	35%	Bachelor's degree
40%	25%	Some post-secondary/college diploma
18%	18%	High school
5%	3%	Less than high school

Source: Institute for Competitiveness & Prosperity analysis based on data from Statistics Canada,
Labour Force Survey; U.S. Census Bureau, U.S. Bureau of Labor Statistics, Current Population Survey.

In 2004 we commissioned research among successful Ontario start-ups – firms that had been initially funded by venture capital and became publicly held or acquired by a public firm.[2] The sample size was small, only twenty-seven; but the results were instructive.

In the survey, we asked about eleven factors generally required in successful companies. For each factor, we asked if the company had good access to it and if it represented an advantage or disadvantage versus their principal competitor – in all cases a U.S.-based firm. Of the eleven, six factors were relatively available in Canada and did not represent a major disadvantage for companies versus their competitors. These were physical infrastructure, qualified scientific or technical

Exhibit 39 **Access to management talent is a key challenge for successful Ontario start-ups**

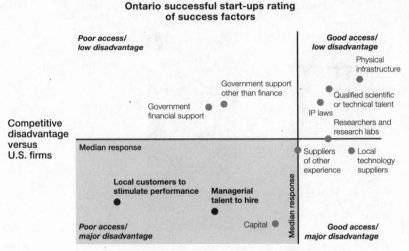

Ontario successful start-ups rating
of success factors

From Institute research among twenty-seven successful venture-backed start-ups.
X-axis: Did respondent report 'poor' access or 'good' access on a 1-to-5 scale to each of the thirteen factors on the graph. Y-axis: Did respondent report 'major disadvantage' or 'low disadvantage' vs. major U.S. competitor (note 'advantage' was a possible response – but average responses were in the disadvantaged area).
Source: The Strategic Counsel, *Assessing the Experience of Successful Innovative Firms in Ontario*, September 2004, a report sponsored by the Institute for Competitiveness & Prosperity, http://www.competeprosper.ca/research/InnovationInterviewStudyRep.pdf.

talent, intellectual-property and patent laws, researchers and research labs, local technology suppliers, and suppliers of other expertise.

Two resources – government financial support and other government support – were not readily available, but did not represent a significant weakness versus competitors. Finally, three of the eleven resources were scarce and represented a major weakness versus competition. Two of these, local customers to stimulate performance and managerial talent to hire, have not been significant targets of public policy, while the third, capital, has been a major priority. The lack of beneficial support from managerial talent is an important gap in the effort to create innovative firms in Canada.

As we have seen, Canada has significantly fewer business graduates than the United States. But this is not a reflection of the lack of demand by Canadian students. Rather, it is because it is more difficult to gain access to a university undergraduate business program than to engineering or arts and science programs.[3]

Overall, a key part of the solution to Canada's lagging prosperity is to upgrade management talent. Management skills are a critical complement to science and engineering skills in creating a high-quality supply of innovation, driving sophisticated demand for innovation, and putting in place the required quantity and quality of financing to make the Innovation System work effectively.

Our colleague Michelle Alexopoulos at the University of Toronto developed a methodology for measuring innovation in management techniques, going as far back as Taylor's *Principles of Scientific Management* published in 1911. Her approach is built on the premise that the development and diffusion of new management techniques, such as just-in-time, lean manufacturing and management by objectives, can be tracked by counting the number of new books in each topic area. As the number grows over time, one can infer greater development of the technique – and check for a relationship with concurrent economic growth.[4] She concludes that increases in the publication of books on management are correlated with growth in productivity and prosperity. Following the introduction of a new management technique that causes a 10 per cent increase in new management books, GDP and productivity grow at statistically significant higher rates than average for approximately six years.[5] It is not a stretch to conclude from this that improved management can have a significant effect on a region's or nation's prosperity.

Canadian Managers' Capabilities Can Be Improved

At the plant level, Canadian manufacturing management is among the world's best, but like other countries we trail the United States[6] (Exhibit 40).

Our management teams are leaders in implementing specific

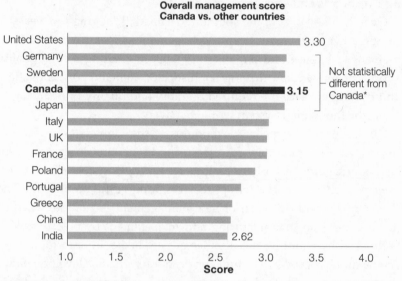

Exhibit 40 **Canada is among the leaders in the overall quality of its manufacturing management but trails the United States significantly**

Overall management score
Canada vs. other countries

* At the 10% significance level.
Source: Institute for Competitiveness & Prosperity, Management matters dataset. For further survey work, see Nick Bloom and John Van Reenen, 'Measuring and Explaining Management Practices Across Firms and Countries,' *Quarterly Journal of Economics*, November 2007.

techniques in the area of lean manufacturing. They are solid perform-ers in effecting good performance management, with some room for improvement. But, while they match management teams in other lead-ing economies in people management, Canadian firms trail U.S. ones significantly. Canada underperforms especially in the willingness of managers to keep and promote high performers and to deal promptly with poor performers.

Our results also indicate that one of the key variables that drives – or at least is correlated with – better management is educational attain-ment of the plant management team. Across the countries surveyed, multinational firms outperform firms that are strictly domestic, and Canada is no exception. Moreover, Canadian-based multinationals that are market leaders globally are among the best managed in the world. Businesses that strive for international success can and do achieve great results.

Management capabilities are important contributors to national prosperity. And our manufacturing management is among the world's best. Nevertheless, our businesses can get better, especially through the advanced education of our management cadre. In fact, it is short-sighted, if not dangerous, for Canada's firms to compete globally with management skills that are not as strong as they can be.

10 Bulk Up, Not Hollow Out

The term 'hollowing out' has gained currency in the past few years. The proponents of the hollowing out 'crisis' have created a nearly universal belief that corporate Canada is being eviscerated by the foreign take-over of our corporations and the export of their head-office functions, with a corresponding loss of our autonomy. As a result, they claim, we are heading toward an economy of branch offices, which is one of the depressing future results of foreign control. For them, the only question now on the table is what our government should do to slow this owner-ship exodus.

Yes, some significant Canadian firms have been taken over by foreign firms – Inco, Falconbridge, Zenon Environmental – to name a few. But do these visible changes really signal a hollowing out of our corporate infrastructure? Or are they just getting noticed more now, just like the attention typically paid to large-scale layoffs even though these are usu-ally more than offset by the unannounced, unpublicized creation of new jobs?

Canada Has a Growing List of Global Leaders

Rather than hollowing out, we find that the number of Canadian com-panies that are global leaders[1] is higher today than twenty years ago. As

Exhibit 41 **As of November 2011 Canada had ninety-four global leaders**

AbitibiBowater	Coastal Contacts	Major Drilling	Sierra Wireless
Ag Growth	Com Dev International	Manulife Financial	SMART Technologies
Agrium	Cott	McCain	SNC-Lavalin
Aimia	DALSA	MDS Nordion	Spectra Premium
Alimentation	Dorel Industries	MEGA Brands	Student Transportation
Couche-Tard	EXCO Technologies	Methanex	SunGro Horticulture
Alliance Grain Traders	EXFO Electro-Optical	Mitel	Superior Plus (ERCO)
Arctic Glacier	Engineering	Neo Material	Targray Technology
ATCO	Finning International	Technologies	TD Ameritrade
ATS	FirstService (Colliers)	Norbord	Teck Resources
Barrick Gold	Fortress Paper	North American Fur	Tembec
Bombardier	Garda World Security	Auctions	The ALDO Group
Brookfield Asset	Gildan	OpenText	The Jim Pattison Group
Management	Goldcorp.	Pan American Silver	Thomson Corporation
CAE	Goodlife Fitness	Pason Systems	TLC Vision
Cameco	Harlequin (Torstar)	Peerless Clothing	Transat A.T.
Canadian National	Héroux-Devtek	Pollard	Trimac
Railway	Husky Injection Molding	PotashCorp	Velan
Canam	(Onex)	Premier Tech	Village Farms
Canfor	IMAX	Research in Motion	Viterra
Catalyst Paper	Lallemand	Ritchie Bros.	Wescast
CCL Industries	Linamar (Skyjack)	Auctioneers	West Fraser Timber
Celestica	Logan International	Royal Bank of Canada	Westport Innovations
Chemtrade Logistics	MAAX (Tricap Partners)	Samuel, Son & Co.	Zarlink
Cinram	Magna	Scotia Mocatta	ZCL Composites
Cirque du Soleil		ShawCor	

Source: Institute for Competitiveness & Prosperity.

of November 2011, Canada had ninety-four global leaders (Exhibit 41), up significantly from thirty-three in 1985.

Canada's list of thirty-three global leaders in 1985 included such firms as Hiram Walker, McCain's, Northern Telecom, Canada Malting, Alcan, Inco, Abitibi-Price, Bombardier, and Laidlaw. The hollowing-out thesis holds that we currently have markedly and worrisomely fewer such firms today because of foreign takeovers, such as those of 1985 leaders Falconbridge, Moore Corp, Seagram's, and Hiram Walker. But the creation of new globally competitive Canadian champions dwarfs the losses.

Our global leaders have higher productivity and greater productivity growth than non-globally competitive companies. They do more R&D

and can afford to invest in larger-scale operations. And Canadian companies that achieve global scale are major wealth creators for Canadians. Of the seventy-five richest Canadians,[2] an impressive 23 per cent were the builders of Canada's global leaders.

Our new global leaders come from many sectors: high tech (ATS Automation Tooling Systems, CAE, Celestica, OpenText, Research In Motion), retail (Couche-Tard), manufacturing (Magna, Husky Injection Molding), financial services (Manulife Financial), information (Thomson Reuters), and health care (TLC Vision), to name but a few. The average Canadian global leader today is much larger than the average leader in 1985 – 78 per cent bigger as defined by sales revenue in constant dollars.

Our global leaders gained their position almost exclusively through innovation. Of the ninety-four current leaders, sixty-eight achieved global leadership through innovative products, services, or processes – Harlequin and its approach to book publishing and marketing, Alimentation Couche-Tard's acquisition and logistics capabilities, or ATCO's construction techniques. One, Neo Materials Technologies, achieved global leadership through pure invention. The remaining twenty-five drew on a combination of invention and innovation – RIM with its wireless-technology patents and its creative approach to distribution, or Dorel Industries with its patented technology and its acquisition strategy.

What, then, are the policy implications? Clearly, we would love both to keep our current globally competitive corporations and to build new ones. No committed Canadian wants to see our globally competitive companies taken over. But we should not stand in the way of foreign investors who are prepared to buy Canadian companies that have not aggressively capitalized on opportunities in their own business. Nor should we be afraid to admit, if reluctantly, that sometimes our Canadian management teams are not up to the challenge of global competition and that new, foreign-based management is needed to face it. And we must recognize that anything we do that would have the effect of slowing the creation of new globally competitive corporations in order to staunch the takeover of existing corporations would do real harm to Canada's prosperity.

For Canadians, it is distressing to see companies like ATI, Alcan, and Zenon Environmental bought by foreigners. But that simply raises the stakes for creating the appropriate balance of support and pressure for innovative, growing companies – our global leaders of the future.

There is no single silver bullet to create more Canadian global leaders. Peter Munk, who put Barrick onto the current list of Canada's global leaders, is probably correct when he asserts that Canadian company executives have to show more fortitude in going global.[3] But they need the help of the Canadian capital markets, which systematically underestimate the risk of Canadian firms staying domestic and overestimate the risk of Canadian firms going global.

What about All the Takeovers?

How does our conclusion on the vibrancy of global leaders square with the reality of so many takeovers of Canadian icons?

Of the fifty-seven major foreign takeovers since 2002[4] for which we have financial information, twenty-nine – or more than half – relied on Canada for the majority of their revenues in the year before they were acquired. These companies had not really ventured outside the Canadian market and in some sense provided relatively easy prey for foreign firms that wanted to grow here. Such domestically focused companies include our major steel companies – Algoma, Dofasco, Harris, and Stelco – and some in consumer goods – E.D. Smith, Lakeport, La Senza, Sleeman, and Vincor (although nearly 50 per cent of this successful wine company's sales were outside Canada when it was acquired).

The second group, comprising twenty-eight companies, was more international in scope, with sales abroad accounting for more than 50 per cent of revenues. Still, fifteen of these twenty-eight were not significant players in their markets. So, while steelmakers Co-Steel and Ipsco sold more than 75 per cent of their output beyond Canada and were sizable companies, with more than $1 billion in annual revenues, they were still minor players in their North American and global markets. Similar situations can be found in the computer industry (Cognos and GEAC) and pharmaceuticals (Axcan). TIR Systems earned 83 per cent of its revenues outside Canada, but this manufacturer of LED-based lighting products had achieved annual revenues of only $15 million and was struggling financially.

The remaining thirteen companies were international players and global leaders – that is, they were one of the five largest in their markets. Of these, three – Four Seasons, Intrawest, and Masonite – are still largely headquartered and managed in Canada but are owned by non-Canadian private-equity investors. Of the other ten, five were large Canadian companies that had ceased to be world-class innovators or simply could not capitalize on their inherent advantage – Domtar, Falconbridge, Geac, GSW, and Moore Wallace.

Only five Canadian-owned, globally competitive companies that were also actively engaged in innovating and upgrading were acquired by foreign entities. ATI, Alcan, Creo, VersaCold, and Zenon were acquired by bigger, broader players – Advanced Micro Devices, Rio Tinto, Kodak, Eimskip, and GE, respectively – that turned their Canadian operations into branch offices.

Clearly, in the global economy, successful companies that have not achieved adequate scale are candidates for takeover by larger predators. And the foreign acquisition of Canadian companies that do not compete globally or stop innovating and upgrading will continue, if not accelerate. Such acquisitions may not be smart decisions on the part of the foreign parent. For example, AMT has already taken two large writedowns of the ATI assets. It is generally recognized that RTZ, by increasing its offering price to ensure that it secured Alcan, significantly overpaid and has since written down those assets by an amount nearly equal to the premium it paid.

Around the world, global players are emerging in more and more industries. As they build out their global footprints, they use their scale economies, deep knowledge, and financial might to buy up national players in various targeted markets as well as international competitors that have under-invested in their global ambitions and fallen behind. In this way, the world is getting spikier not flatter, with fewer major global players in each industry rather than numerous national players spread evenly across the globe. In this respect, Canada is experiencing acquisitions that differ only a little from those in other countries.

To many Canadians, it is sad when a brilliant up-and-comer like ATI, which had achieved a leading share in its industry niche of graphic computer chips, gets swallowed up by a big logic-chip maker; or when a great Canadian icon like Alcan, which had grown aggressively both organically and by acquisitions to be among the top aluminum producers in the world, gets taken out by one of the world's two broad-based mining behemoths.

However, Canadians need to remember how some Americans reacted when Canadian National acquired Illinois Central, for whom Abraham Lincoln famously acted as a lawyer, and the iconic name disappeared from the railroad business; or how the British responded when Thomson Corporation announced the acquisition of Reuters, the second-ranked financial-information-services provider in the world, and by doing so converted it into a subsidiary of a Canadian-owned company.

Reciprocity Should Guide Our Foreign Investment Policies

Nevertheless, many are still concerned about the loss to our Canadian economy when foreigners take over our companies. While we are less troubled by the foreign takeovers than many advocates, we do see a role for public policy in assessing takeovers.

Sadly, the federal government's decision in 2011 to block the purchase of Potash Corporation by BHP Billiton is likely to hurt the future competitiveness of Canadian companies. This does not imply that Canada has no right or cause to challenge foreign takeovers of Canadian companies. Far from it. The problem is with the *net benefit* theory and rationale used by our government to block the takeover.

The Investment Canada Act is intended to ensure that foreign direct investment in Canada provides a net benefit to Canada, but it never defines the terms. Instead, it directs the minister of industry to consider several factors related to economic activity, such as productivity, competition, and so on. Suffice to say, there is no certainty about how the minister will determine specific cases.

If net benefit were used in merchandise trade, there would never be a lowering of trade barriers, because every single industry or company that is adversely affected would wrap itself in the protective flag of net benefit. For example, Quebec textile makers would declare there to be no net benefit to allowing free trade in textiles, and Washington State sawmills would declare there to be no net benefit in allowing free trade in softwood lumber.

If our policy remained based on net benefits, other countries would start using net-benefits logic against Canadian companies when they attempt to grow globally through foreign acquisition. And unfortunately, net benefits is such a vague and subjective concept that every single foreign takeover here or abroad can be struck down if the government in question wants to show that there are no net benefits.

In contrast to the net-benefit approach to FDI, merchandise trade policy is based on the theory of *reciprocity*: you let us send you our Black-Berrys without tariffs or restrictions, and we will let in your GE MRI machines. We need to move policy from net benefit to reciprocity as the defining criterion.

The world has moved to freer trade through reciprocity. Nations understand that there will be some net beneficiaries and net benefactors, but that overall there will be an efficiency gain for both economies, so it is sensible to put up with the minuses. It was not at all pleasant to have RTZ buy Alcan and turn it into a tightly managed subsidiary. But it was critical that the United Kingdom allow Thomson to buy Reuters. It was not a highlight to have the U.S. firm AMD buy our ATI, but our

Couche-Tard needed to be allowed to buy Circle K of the United States to become an international heavyweight in convenience-store retailing. That is reciprocity in action.

We are in the middle of a historic fifty-year reshuffling of the ownership of the world's business assets, making international capital flows centrally important to long-term country competitiveness. Around the world, national franchise companies (such as Labatt) are being bought up by global players (Interbrew). And smaller or narrower global players (Zenon Environmental or Falconbridge) are being bought up by bigger or broader global players (GE and Xtrata, respectively).

For this reason, Canada needs to bring the sophistication of the long-established practices from merchandise trade to the realm of foreign takeovers. We need our Canadian companies to globalize without being hobbled by government policies. And we cannot be naive while this is all transpiring.

Basing our policy on reciprocity, not net benefits, is essential to the desired long-term outcome. But it is not reciprocity to allow Vale to buy Inco. The Brazilian government has the absolute right to stop any takeover of Vale. Reciprocity would mean that, if Vale has the right to buy Inco, then Inco would have the right to buy Vale. Similarly, it is not reciprocity to allow BHP to buy Potash. As part of the earlier BHP-Billiton merger, the Australian government imposed draconian restrictions on BHP, meaning that BHP can go hunting internationally but itself can never be hunted.

In this case, the approach that would have protected Canadian competitiveness would have been to allow the Potash takeover with two conditions. The first condition would be that the Australian government remove all restrictions on the foreign takeover of BHP – and prove it by allowing a subsequent standstill period that would enable Potash to put together a consortium to bid for BHP. To be sure, the size of BHP means that this would not likely have occurred, but it would have nevertheless been an important signal of the Australian government's seriousness. The second condition would be that the Australian government sign an agreement binding it not to block any acquisition of an Australian company by a Canadian company. In addition, there could be mutual agreement to exclude certain sectors or to enforce certain requirements post-acquisition, just as we would find in merchandise trade agreements. That would be the first of what would become a series of free FDI agreements.

Despite the prevailing worry by many that Canada is losing our global leaders, it's not true. But our businesses have to be more intent on achieving global leadership status – because foreign takeovers will continue. Our successful start-ups need to look to foreign markets earlier rather than later.

11 Become a True Trading Nation

One way to strengthen innovation performance in Canada is to embrace *freer trade* with as many countries as is practical. International trade drives both support and pressure for innovation. On the support side, it increases market opportunities for our innovators, thereby strengthening the economics of investment. It also increases access to more sophisticated supply chains for our Canadian companies. On the pressure side, imports create the necessity for innovation to ensure survival by our Canadian firms.

Countries like China and India are moving toward an innovation tipping point. Currently, they compete internationally on the basis of low-cost labour and unsophisticated systems. However, at some point in their development, these economies will have more innovative firms; at the same time, their consumers will become more sophisticated and because of their sheer numbers will be important deciders of styles and trends around the world. For Canada to increase its standard of living, we need to ensure that we aspire to be a highly innovative economy. More trade now will help bring the necessary support and pressure.

Traditionally, Trade Is an Engine of Economic Prosperity

From our early days of shipping furs and timber to the Old World through to our current status as a leading exporter of automotive parts and vehicles, Canada's well-being has been inextricably linked to international trade. As developing economies strengthen their capabilities, trade is increasing. Yet the current economic weaknesses have hurt trade and increased the spectre of protectionism. Canada needs to step up efforts to expand trade – to raise innovation and prosperity performance.

Generations of economists have analyzed and assessed the impact and effects of trade. Economic theory has evolved from Adam Smith's insight that trade facilitates specialization, to David Ricardo's theory of comparative advantage, to Eli Heckscher's and Bertil Ohlin's factor-endowments model, to Nobel Laureate Paul Krugman's model of two-way trade in varieties, and to Elhanan Helpman's model of international technology diffusion. Over the centuries, economists have concluded that there are many ways that international trade enhances domestic competitiveness, improves productivity, increases sales, raises real wages, and provides consumers with more product choices at lower prices. Many of them have also highlighted that there are winners and losers from international trade, so that redistributive government policies must be used to ensure that the prosperity from international trade flows broadly to all members of society.

Today, it is almost universally accepted among economists that freer trade has a positive impact on society.[1] In an environment that encourages trade, we can reap the rewards of international technology exchanges and low-wage markets to improve global competition. Ultimately, these benefits translate into more choices and lower prices for consumers; as well, they improve general well-being. Thanks to trade with the United States, Canadians enjoy sophisticated high-tech computer systems; thanks to trade with China, Canadians enjoy low-cost clothing.

But it is fashionable to dismiss the benefits of lower-cost imports because of lost jobs. A typical comment came from Barack Obama when he was a candidate in the 2008 election campaign: '... people don't want a cheaper T-shirt if they're losing a job in the process. They would rather have the job and pay a little bit more for a T-shirt.' However, as Daniel Griswold of the Cato Institute pointed out, 'every poor family must buy those shirts to keep themselves clothed, yet only one-third of 1 percent of American workers make clothing or textiles of any kind. A wealthy ... commentator need not care about the price of a T-shirt or other everyday consumer items, but millions of poor and middle class ... families do care.'[2]

Still, with rising demand, global trade continues to expand and evolve rapidly. This reality is based on sophisticated production techniques, advanced transportation networks, transnational corporations, outsourcing of manufacturing and services, fast development of information communications technology, and rapid industrialization. Growing global trade contributes to nations' prosperity.

Not all agree that the growth of global trade is inevitable. According to Jeff Rubin, former chief economist of CIBC World Markets, as the global economy recovers from recession, markets will once again have to adjust to triple-digit oil prices. With the combination of the return of demand for oil to pre-recession levels and falling supplies, trade in goods and services is about to get substantially more localized. Add to that the high cost of extracting oil from resources, such Alberta's oil sands, as well as increased demand from emerging markets, OPEC's cannibalization of its output as a result of economic growth, and the growing demand for energy-intensive water-desalination projects, and double-digit oil prices may very well be a thing of the past.[3] Rubin concludes that persistent triple-digit oil prices will add significant costs to everything from manufacturing to transportation. As the price of both making and transporting goods increases, access to far-off and foreign markets will fall, making your next-door neighbour an even more important trading partner.

Hal Sirkin and his colleagues at Boston Consulting Group conclude that rising wages and salaries along with transportation costs will shrink China's advantage versus the United States in manufacturing. Add to that the increased domestic demand for China's output, and the authors see a resurgence in U.S. manufacturing in the coming years.

Lower-cost economies like Vietnam and Indonesia will take up some of the production, but their infrastructure and capabilities are not at China's level yet.[4]

Trade Fosters Support and Pressure for Prosperity

Our support and pressure framework is useful in considering the benefits of trade. International trade provides both specialized support and competitive pressure to enhance Canada's productivity and innovative capacity. Productivity improvements enable firms to grow at home and to compete internationally. More important, rising productivity and innovation are the wellspring of broad-based prosperity and the key paths toward national well-being. So it is helpful to understand how international trade affects the pressure and support faced by firms in Canada.

Trade Supports Productivity and Innovation

The small market size of Canada is an ongoing challenge to raising our productivity and advancing innovation. It makes little sense for Canadian firms to invest large amounts of money in R&D or raise capital for our small market alone. Trade increases the size of markets available to support our firms. This is a key reason why exporting to the United States has been so important to the success of our firms. Canada still suffers from smaller scale in our manufacturing, but it would be worse without Canada-U.S. free trade. The impact of increasing scale by adding U.S. as well as other international customers to our market justifies large innovation investments and gives creative firms the opportunity to succeed. In addition, international markets expose Canadian firms to sophisticated suppliers of specialized inputs, including machinery and services related to research and financing.[5]

Trade Pressures Productivity and Innovation

Trade strengthens the pressure on our firms, workers, and managers.

When foreign firms export to Canada or establish production facilities here, they increase this competitive pressure on Canadian firms. Opening our markets to more rivals creates an uncomfortable situation – our firms must ensure they are competing effectively or close up shop. The most familiar form of pressure is cost-based, such as from Walmart or Target expanding to Canada, or Chinese toy manufacturers flooding our markets with their exports. But the more subtle and ultimately more important form of pressure is innovation-based, as when Apple enters the smart-phone market and challenges Research In Motion to take its product innovations to a new level.

Trade also exposes our firms to more sophisticated customers outside Canada who care about costs and quality, forcing our firms to compete on the basis of innovation. To be sure, trade, and all forms of pressure, have a 'dark side' in that they force the less innovative and unproductive firms to improve their performance or go out of business.

Freer Trade Strengthens Support and Pressure

A University of Toronto economist and a colleague of ours, Professor Daniel Trefler, analyzed the impact of the Canada-U.S. Free Trade Agreement of 1989 and concluded that the real-world results were consistent with academic theories.[6] He showed the downside of increased pressure, as the fall in the Canadian tariff forced many import-competing Canadian plants to contract and even close their doors. About 100,000 workers were forced to look elsewhere for employment. Fortunately, most found jobs in export-oriented plants, so that unemployment rates did not rise and wages did not fall.

But the upside of support was far larger – in the form of improved access to U.S. markets. As Canadian firms expanded into the U.S. market, average Canadian productivity rose by an astounding 8 per cent. Why? The tariff changes led to the growth of the most productive firms and to the contraction of the least-productive ones. The mechanism is similar to that of a student who has written two tests and is suddenly allowed to put more weight on the better test – the average grade rises.

Support also had another positive impact. In preparation for expansion into the U.S. market, Canadian firms engaged in a series of productivity-enhancing activities: they invested in developing new products and processes, they adopted state-of-the-art advanced manufacturing technologies, and they invested in worker-training programs. The result was that the typical Canadian plant increased its productivity by 5 per cent. Adding this to the previous 8 per cent gain led to overall productivity gains of 13 per cent. The fact that a simple government policy of reducing tariffs could raise manufacturing productivity by 13 per cent is truly remarkable.

As further evidence, economists Philippe Aghion and Peter Howitt have made the correlation between innovation and trade, concluding that more access to foreign markets supports domestic innovators by increasing the size of markets available to them. It also pressures domestic innovation laggards to innovate more, through greater market competition from foreign producers who compete with domestic producers. This forces the less innovative and unproductive firms out of the market and pressures those who survive to innovate so they can continue to be successful in the more competitive environment created by openness to trade.[7]

More access to foreign markets and free trade increase innovation, which in turn raises productivity. This is an important issue for Canada. Time and time again, our analyses have shown that lagging productivity is a major contributor to the prosperity gap between Canada and the United States. More trade means a more prosperous Canada.

Emerging Economies' Trade Is Approaching a Tipping Point

Emerging economies evolve to reach an innovation tipping point.[8] Low-cost-based economies are those that depend on the low cost of labour and natural resources to compete globally. Innovation-based economies are driven by skilled labour to create unique and high-value-added goods and services, thus creating a competitive advantage. The tipping point is the term that describes the moment when an economy evolves from low-cost competition to innovation-based competition. For that to occur, two conditions must be satisfied.

The first is the development of sophisticated institutions. They are needed to secure, facilitate, and encourage investment and innovation. Property-rights institutions, such as the rule of law and well-developed contract enforcement by civil authorities, are needed to protect investors from arbitrary expropriation by government officials. A sophisticated financial network is needed to facilitate the flow of capital from those who have it to those who need it. A transparent and accessible legal system is needed to govern relations between firms and, in particular, to protect the intellectual property that results from investments in innovation. It is also imperative that creativity is supported by a national innovation system that includes patent offices, patent courts, and world-class universities. These institutions support innovation.

The second condition is the presence of sophisticated consumers together with intense competition. They are a necessity for continued pressure for more innovation. The more sophisticated consumers are, the better the goods and services they will expect. And the more competitive the business environment, the more firms will be forced to cater to sophisticated demand. This is a key driver of the location of R&D, design, and other creative elements in an economy. Most of the world's richest economies have succeeded by competing on the basis of creativity and sophistication; they have long ago ceased relying on low wages or natural resources as their source of competitive advantage.

Once the institutional support and the intense and sophisticated demand pressure are in place, an economy can make the transition from a low-cost-based global competitor to an innovation-based global competitor. These ideas provide a rich framework for thinking about how emerging economies like China and India will affect Canada.

Currently, the most sophisticated consumers are concentrated in the OECD countries. We expect this dynamic to continue to change over time, as the standard of living of consumers in China and India improves and they begin to apply pressure on organizations to accommodate their growing needs.[9] Already Chinese and Indian customers are demanding innovative goods, such as China's Chery and India's Tata cars.[10] But to date, China and India have not moved from competing on the basis of low wages to innovation and sophistication.[11] When there are enough sophisticated consumers in China and India to support domestic firms, coupled with investment in innovation-sustaining institutions, these countries will have reached the tipping point.

Once they move past the tipping point, world leadership in innovation will begin to shift away from the developed economies of the OECD to China and India. When this happens, many Chinese and Indian firms will have unplugged themselves from their past and become significant competitors to every profitable corporation in the industrialized world.[12]

Canadians cannot control or stall the spectacular growth of innovative capability in China and India. But we can stimulate the growth of our own innovative capacity. As we have seen, Canadian innovation presents a mixed picture. While we are home to many world-leading companies, Canadian business-sector indicators of innovation, such as R&D and patenting, are among the lowest in the OECD and are far lower than those in the United States.

If we do not want China and India to crowd us out of the OECD innovation leaders group, then we will have to stop worrying about what we cannot control and start taking major steps toward drastically improving our own innovative capacity. We can choose reactive complacency, or we can choose to push forward with a set of active and positive innovation policies. The choice is ours to make, but we must make it now – China and India will not wait.

China's Impact on Our Economy Is Still Minimal

While several countries are emerging economically, China's remarkable progress is probably the most important development in these early years of the twenty-first century. Through sweeping reforms in its economic structures, China has leapt forward in its prosperity and its presence in international markets.

But has China reached the innovation tipping point – the point at which it competes on the basis of world-class innovation capabilities instead of low-cost labour? We conclude that it has not yet reached this milestone. Its manufactured goods seem to be everywhere, and they are becoming more and more sophisticated; yet China is still assembling the technology of others and is not creating high value in its own operations. It is investing significantly in research and development; yet its patents tend to be more imitative than inventive. China is producing many engineers; yet many of these are lower skilled than their counterparts in other countries. The country is booming with opportunity; yet there has not been a mass return of Chinese students educated abroad, as seen in other innovative economies. Its institutions are being reformed to support innovation; yet much needs to be done to resolve internal conflicts between a market economy and an authoritarian regime.

We are by no means suggesting that we can be complacent in Canada. To date, China has expanded its economy and competed on the world stage as a low-cost competitor. So far, China's trade has not had a significant negative effect on Canada's economy. However, in time, its innovation capacity will develop further, and China will become a more sophisticated competitor to our businesses and people. So Canada needs to step up its innovation capabilities now.

How has China's emergence as an economic powerhouse played out in Canada? Has our trade relationship benefited or harmed our businesses and workers? China is not the primary cause of our current weakness in manufacturing employment; instead, our appreciating exchange rate is a more important factor.

Many of us perceive that China has a bigger impact on our economy than is the reality. In the Schmidts' house there are many items with the 'Made in China' label – toys and games, the family computer and its peripherals, and clothing. This is because China's highest-volume exports to Canada tend to be consumer goods. While we see these items daily in our homes and in stores, many other items are as important in our lives and our economy. The Schmidts and other Canadians are not confronted with a 'Made in China' label on the sophisticated control devices for their heating and air conditioning; nor do they see this label on their drug prescriptions or savings accounts; nor on the advanced machinery that guides our factories. These services, commodities, and intermediate goods make up a high percentage of our economic lives and affect employment. But their country of origin is largely invisible.

Coincident with the dramatic and visible growth of imports to Canada from China, manufacturing employment in Canada has been in steep decline – more than 300,000 jobs were lost between 2002 and 2008. Yet the causal connection between these two trends is not as high as some would think. The strengthening of the Canadian dollar over that period has been much more of a factor in the decline in manufacturing employment. As our dollar strengthened, our exports became more expensive and imports less expensive, thus hurting firms that compete internationally. In addition, while we have had periods of growth in the past decades, manufacturing's share of employment has been falling over the long run – as it has in all other advanced economies and China (Exhibit 42).

Where we do see a connection between imports from China and losses in Canadian manufacturing employment, it has been in low-value-added industries like textiles. In fact, parts of Canada's manufacturing sector are growing, and these tend to be the higher-value, more sophisticated industries like production machinery and medical devices (Exhibit 43). The manufacturing industries that grew while the overall sector was in decline had higher productivity and drew more on creativity-oriented occupations – Richard Florida's creative class.

The solution for those worried about imports from China and elsewhere is not trade barriers or a higher-value yuan. It is, instead, the relentless pursuit of innovation and creativity by our manufacturers. Across the breadth of our economy, it is very difficult to conclude that

Exhibit 42 **Across the developed economies and China, manufacturing has declined as a share of total employment**

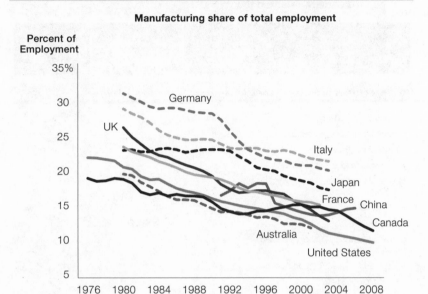

Manufacturing share of total employment

Note: For United States, it is manufacturing employment share out of total non-farm employees.
Source: Institute for Competitiveness & Prosperity analysis based on data from Statistics Canada; U.S. Bureau of Labor Statistics; OECD STAN Indicators database, 2006; China Statistical Yearbook 2008, http://www.bls.gov/fls/chinareport.pdf.

China's growth has hurt our overall employment results. Imports from China have been growing in Canada in this decade, but until the current recession our employment performance has been robust. Our recent slowdown is more the result of global factors, particularly in the United States, than of Chinese competition.

The European Union Is Canada's Trade Opportunity

The European Union (EU) is our second most important trading partner after the United States, and this relationship has been growing. While China represents opportunities for increased trade as it becomes more developed, the EU is already a large and sophisticated

Exhibit 43 **Most manufacturing industries lost jobs, 2002–8; growing industries had higher-value-added and more creativity-oriented jobs**

NAICS4	Share of net change in jobs (2002–8)	Value added per employee, weighted by employment change	Occupational mix, 2002
Manufacturing industries losing jobs			**Mix of jobs**
Cut and Sew Clothing	-13%		Creativity-oriented 16%
Sawmills and Wood Preservation	-8		
Motor Vehicle Parts	-7		
Pulp, Paper, and Paperboard Mills	-6		
Household and Institutional Furniture and Kitchen Cabinets	-5		
Rubber Products	-4	**$88,400**	Routine-oriented, physical 68%
Motor Vehicles	-4		
Semi-conductor and Other Electronic Components	-4		
Printing and Related Support Activities	-4		
Clothing Knitting Mills	-3		
Foundries	-3		
Iron and Steel Mills and Ferro-Alloys	-3		Routine-oriented, service 16%
Other 56 industries	-50		
Manufacturing industries gaining jobs			**Mix of jobs**
Agricultural, Construction, and Mining Machinery	2		Creativity-oriented 25%
Other Foods	2		
Architectural and Structural Metals	2		
Pharmaceuticals and Medicines	1	**$110,000**	Routine-oriented, physical 53%
Cement and Concrete Products	1		
Other General-Purpose Machinery	1		
Petroleum and Coal Products	1		
Medical Equipment and Supplies	1		Routine-oriented, service 22%
Other 10 industries	3		

Total manufacturing jobs lost, net   315,000

Note: Our analysis by NAICS4 is based on the Survey of Employment, Payroll and Hours (SEPH) dataset, which is Canada's only source of detailed information at the industry level. SEPH data provide information related to jobs based on a census of administration data from businesses.
Source: Institute for Competitiveness & Prosperity analysis based on data from Industry Canada.

trade partner. Expanding our trade with this innovation-based economic region can also increase the support and competitive pressure for our businesses, since consumer preferences and institutions there are familiar to us, while offering us the support of well-developed market opportunities. The sophisticated European consumer can provide beneficial pressure on our businesses to strengthen their product and service offerings even more. The competitive pressure from European imports can also stimulate more innovation in Canada.

The EU's importance as a trade partner has increased in recent years, both in terms of the share of total Canadian imports and as a share of total exports. With the United States experiencing economic difficulties, the case for an expanded EU trade relationship is strong – for its immediate economic benefits and as a means of expanding and diversifying our trade. Negotiations for expanded trade between Canada and the EU are under way. While it is unfortunate that harmful barriers in our two economies' agricultural sectors will not be dismantled in these negotiations, it is quite encouraging that we are pursuing this important initiative for strengthening our innovation capabilities. Our federal and provincial government leaders should be congratulated. Our businesses must pursue the resulting opportunities available to them.

Protectionism Is in Fashion and We Have to Resist It

Much of the current economic debate revolves around how we can get back to economic growth and repair our governments' fiscal house. What is equally important, however, is the need to tackle protectionist threats and increase global trade.

Protectionism contributed mightily to the collapse of global trade from U.S. $5.3 billion in 1929 to U.S. $1.8 billion by 1933. This is a key reason why the Depression was so deep and long – and we can't forget this lesson. While protectionist measures may be politically popular, they will only lengthen the recession and leave us all worse off.

Today, we are hearing the siren call of protectionism, led by voices in the United States. Seductive arguments about saving jobs and standing up against currency 'manipulation' and 'unfair' trade practices have resurfaced and rebounded around the world. During the 2008–9 recession, the U.S. government adopted 'Buy American' policies. Among other things, its stimulus legislation required that iron, steel, and manufactured goods used in projects it funded be produced domestically. The United States also increased tariffs on tires from China, which then placed tariffs on U.S. nylon, though it did not indicate that this was in direct retaliation. Further escalating the trade row, China levied tariffs of nearly 100 per cent on U.S. poultry products.

The recent ratification of U.S. trade deals with Colombia, Panama, and South Korea is a positive development, but the 'Buy American' sentiment is alive and well.

Nor is protectionism confined to the United States. In Europe, French President Nicolas Sarkozy asserted in 2010 that, if his government were to give financial aid to the country's ailing auto sector, he didn't want to see another factory built in the Czech Republic. The Slovakian prime minister countered that, if the French were to make good on their threat, he would 'send Gaz de France home.'

We see mixed signals in Canada. On a positive note, encouraged by Ontario and Quebec, the federal government is negotiating freer trade with the EU. And the Federation of Canadian Municipalities decided not to urge its member municipalities to stop purchasing goods and services from the United States. This helped buy time for Canadian and American government talks on exempting Canada from the 'Buy American' policy.

On the negative side, Ontario's Green Energy Act requires subsidized wind and solar projects to abide by local content rules, attracting objections to the World Trade Organization (WTO) from Japan, the EU, and the United States. The Quebec government passed legislation in October 2010 to ensure that Bombardier participates in the manufacture of new subway cars for Montreal's transit system.

The prevailing view, then, is that exports are good because they increase jobs and imports are bad because they cost jobs. But imports are critical for a healthy economy. At the very least, one has to accept imports as we bargain with other countries to increase our exports. Prime Minister R.B. Bennett promised that he would get Canada out of the 1930s Depression by 'blasting' Canadian exports into world markets while imposing import tariffs. That didn't turn out so well.

Imports are more than a necessary evil. They benefit consumers. They help our businesses become more innovative and productive through support and pressure. While trade overall is a positive economic force, our trade balance – the difference between exports and imports – is not that important. Canada typically has a trade surplus, but its magnitude in any given year between 1980 and 2009 had no meaningful relationship with GDP growth. The United States has had only trade deficits over the same period, with no relationship between the size of its annual deficit and GDP growth. Mexico has had both trade deficits and surpluses, but the relationship is the opposite of what protectionists would argue – increased deficits are associated with higher GDP growth and increased surpluses with lower GDP growth. It's difficult to make the case that trade deficits hurt our economic prospects.

Canada has closed or is pursuing several free-trade deals with other countries and so we're on the right track. We think it would be better to focus our negotiating efforts on fewer bigger partners than the several small deals we are now negotiating. We also think that trade negotiations represent a great opportunity to shed ourselves of supply-management policies in many of our agriculture products. Our policy of restricting supply through quotas in dairy products, poultry, and other agricultural goods keeps prices artificially high, protects the income of our famers, and stifles innovation. It also means that potential international trade deals cannot be negotiated because foreign governments rightly object to their agricultural products being kept out of Canada. The federal government has suggested that Canada can successfully take part in Asian free-trade negotiations and main-

tain supply management. We're skeptical we can achieve this, and we
hope we opt for trade over supply management.

*International trade presents a great opportunity for Canada's leadership. We
have begun a process for liberalizing trade with the European Union and
others, and we should pursue this purposefully. While China and India are
relatively insignificant trade partners for us now, more trade with them will
help secure our long-term prosperity.*

*Still, our largest trading partner will continue to be the United States,
regardless of our success in deepening other relationships. We need to resist
impulses to strike back at 'Buy American.' Our diplomatic efforts have to focus
on securing preferred treatment and, better yet, reminding our friends in the
United States and around the world of the importance of expanded international trade.*

12 Focus on Poverty, Not Inequality

If you ask him, Michael Schmidt would say he has never experienced poverty. As for Maria, while she has never really thought about it, she and her family definitely had challenges making ends meet when her parents first moved to Canada. In their married life, however, she and Michael have never been poor. One or both of them were always employed. The Schmidt family has been in the top fifth of household income since Maria started teaching again.

As we'll see, single parents are more likely to be in poverty and Sandra is no exception at this point in her life. Kevin's university degree and early employment success make his current and future prospects for avoiding poverty look good. Louise has not graduated from high school yet. But, assuming she does graduate and moves on to post-secondary education, Louise, too, has a good chance of avoiding poverty.

The Schmidts' history and current situation point to important questions in any discussions about raising Canada's economic performance. Does improving Canada's competitiveness mean that the gains accrue only to those who are already earning the highest income? Does the economic success of one person come at the expense of others – a zero-sum game? If we adopt the policies we are recommending for greater competiveness, will that mean more poverty? These are all fair questions, and they deserve answers.

Our work on prosperity, poverty, and inequality indicates that poverty is concentrated among specific groups in our population who are being excluded from contributing to and sharing in increased prosperity. As we'll show, this exclusion is not the result of a grand conspiracy or a structural defect in our economy. In most cases, the world is changing quickly, and those who lack the right skills are being left behind. Rising income inequality has been the norm in recent decades across developed economies, including Canada's. But it is incorrect to say that higher prosperity is driving greater inequality. The two trends are not related. The more important consideration is the incidence of poverty, which is not the same as increased inequality. We have several observations on this difference.

First, our research has revealed that poverty is not distributed randomly throughout society. It falls mainly on six specific high-risk groups – high school dropouts, lone parents, persons with disabilities, unattached individuals between the ages of forty-five and sixty-four, recent immigrants, and Aboriginal people.

The percentage of the population living below the Low-Income Cut-Off (LICO) is a measure of poverty in Canada. LICO is defined as the income levels at which persons or families spend a greater proportion – twenty percentage points or more – of their total income on food, shelter, and clothing than the average family of similar size.[1] This can be measured on the basis of income from wages and investment plus government transfers – total income – or after taxes and transfer income. LICO is an imperfect indicator of poverty because it doesn't directly measure deprivation or allow for differences in costs of living across communities and provinces. But LICO can be used at a community level and it does allow for trends over time.

The likelihood of after-tax income falling below LICO increases significantly for individuals who are in the risk groups we identified above. Much of the challenge they face is gaining more attachment to the labour force. The probability of earning income below LICO increases dramatically for each risk group when these individuals are unemployed. The probability also increases when other risk-group members are also high school dropouts (Exhibit 44).

Second, the measures of inequality and poverty are different. The Gini coefficient measures income inequality across a group of people. A

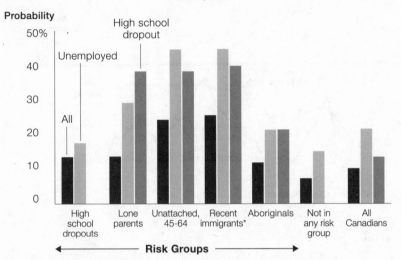

Exhibit 44 **Likelihood of being below LICO is higher for
certain risk groups**

Probability of after-tax income below Low Income Cut-Off
Canada, 2005

* Ten years or fewer.
Note: Probabilities based on regression for working age 25–64, controlling for age, age-squared, marital
status, education, and membership in other risk groups. 'All' refers to the members of the specified risk
group – controlling for membership in other risk groups. Data for disabled not available.
Source: Institute for Competitiveness & Prosperity analysis based on data from Statistics Canada, 2006
Census microdata.

Gini coefficient of 0 means that all people earn exactly the same income,
while a measure of 1 means that one person receives all the income.
These are extremes that are never found anywhere. Actual measures
are typically between 0.3 and 0.5. The higher the Gini coefficient, the
greater the inequality.

Third, we see that broad-based inequality, as measured by the Gini
coefficient, has not been closely related to poverty rates, as measured
by the percentage of the population below the after-tax LICO. Government tax and transfer polices reduce inequality and for this reason we
should focus on the after-tax measure. By either measure, inequality
had been trending upward between 1980 and 2000 but has been flat
since then (Exhibit 45). Poverty rates appear to be much more cyclical
– they rose in the early 1980s following the recession and fell through

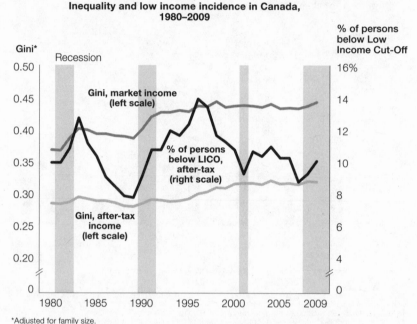

Exhibit 45 **Inequality has remained fairly flat in recent years; poverty has changed with economic cycles**

Inequality and low income incidence in Canada, 1980–2009

*Adjusted for family size.
Source: Institute for Competitiveness & Prosperity analysis based on data from Statistics Canada.

the balance of the decade before turning up in the early 1990s as the economy went through another recession. Poverty rates grew through much of that decade before starting to decline in 1997. Between 2001 and 2009, poverty rates were below the average for the past twenty years, while inequality was at its highest.

Poverty Is Higher among High-Risk Groups

As noted above, poverty is not distributed randomly. Not surprisingly, people with low incomes – including the six groups of Canadians that are much more likely to be below LICO – are over-represented in the bottom of the income distribution:[2]

- high school dropouts;
- lone parents – most frequently mothers;
- persons with disabilities;
- individuals aged between forty-five and sixty-four who are living alone ('unattached');
- recent immigrants – those who have immigrated in the last ten years; and
- Aboriginal people.

An individual in one or more of these groups is 3.3 times as likely as other Canadians to have income (after taxes and transfers) that is inadequate to afford the necessities of life. Within these risk groups, unattached individuals aged forty-five to sixty-four and recent immigrants have the highest incidence of income below LICO.

Our analysis of the data from the 2006 Census indicates that, for those forty-five- to sixty-four-year-olds, living alone is associated with a 25 per cent probability of having income below LICO. Unattached individuals in this age group who did not obtain a high school diploma experience an even higher probability – 39 per cent – of being below LICO. Recent immigrants were close behind in the risk of falling below LICO (Exhibit 44).

Aboriginal people and high school dropouts were slightly better off; the probability of individuals in these two groups being below LICO is 11 to 13 per cent, controlling for other risk factors. Unfortunately, our data source, the Canadian Census, does not measure incomes of persons with disabilities – but they are overrepresented in the bottom of the income distribution.

The probabilities of earning income below LICO increase dramatically for each risk group when the individuals are also high school dropouts. High school dropouts who are not members of these other risk groups have a relatively low likelihood of being below LICO. However, for those who are in the other risk groups, their probability of earning income below LICO increases substantially.

Canadians who are not in any of these risk groups are much less likely to live in poverty, as measured by LICO – with the probability being below 7 per cent in 2005. Clearly, this is too high, but the data indicate that poverty is highly concentrated across these identifiable risk groups, and we need to ensure that poverty-fighting initiatives are aimed at the specific challenges they face.

Some generalizations are warranted. Given that employment reduces the probability of being below LICO, public policy needs to aim at ensuring that members of these risk groups are working. And the importance of a high school diploma is heightened for members of these risk groups.

From the perspective of inequality, the same pattern emerges. The six high-risk groups are heavily concentrated in the bottom quintiles of income distribution. Fully 36 per cent of lone parents have after-tax, after-transfer earnings that place them in the bottom quintile of Ontario's distribution. Two-thirds are in the bottom two quintiles.

Other risk groups exhibit similar patterns (Exhibit 46). As with incidence below LICO, high school dropouts do not fare as badly as the other risk groups; still, 59 per cent of them are in the bottom two quintiles of the distribution of income after tax and government transfers.

For the 62 per cent of Canadians who are not in any of these risk groups, a relatively small percentage find themselves in the bottom of the income distribution. In 2005, just under 13 per cent of these individuals were in the bottom quintile of income distribution. By contrast, half were in the top two quintiles.

These results are consistent for the different definitions of income (market income only, market income plus transfer income, and, as shown in Exhibit 46, after-tax, after-transfer income) and for the Census years 1980, 1990, and 2000.

Each risk group presents its own set of challenges for public policy.

High School Dropouts Face Growing Challenges in a More Sophisticated Economy

The Schmidts recognized the importance of education and always assumed that their children would finish high school – at a bare minimum. Still, too many families over the years have not insisted that their

Exhibit 46 **Members of high-risk groups tend to be in lower-income quintiles**

Distribution of adult-equivalent total income (after tax and transfers)
Canada, 2005

Percentage of
individuals

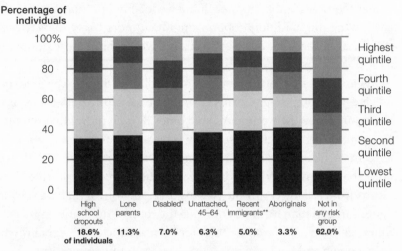

* Income after transfers before tax for the disabled. Disabled excludes those with 'mild' disabilities.
** Ten years or fewer.
Note: Includes both census families and unattached individuals; adult-equivalent family income defined as family income over the square root of family size; main earner (except for disabled) of age 25 to 64.
Source: Institute for Competitiveness & Prosperity analysis based on data from Statistics Canada, 2006 Census microdata and 2006 Participation and Activity Limitation Survey.

children complete high school. People without a high school diploma account for 19 per cent of all Canadians.

By itself, lacking a high school diploma is not the factor most directly related to low income. But members of other risk groups who are also high school dropouts perform worse economically than those who have completed high school (Exhibit 48). As measured by the probability of being in the bottom one or two quintiles and being below LICO, high school dropouts' performance has deteriorated most steadily over the last decades. Sandra Schmidt falls into the category of lone parents, and her economic hardships reflect this. Her situation would likely be even worse if she lacked a high school diploma.

Lifetime employment earnings are lower for those who lack a high school diploma. They are also much more likely to feel the sting of unemployment generally and more so during recessions.

Our analysis of the 2003 International Adult Literacy and Skills survey indicates that high school dropouts have the least-developed skills among the risk groups. In prose literacy, document literacy, and problem solving, high school dropouts are much more likely to be in low-skill cohorts, and their average scores are well behind those of the rest of the population.

One area of hope for dropouts is in the skilled trades. The evidence indicates that high school dropouts who successfully gain trade certification improve their economic outcomes. For an individual who has not completed high school, securing a trade certificate adds about 20 per cent to his or her annual income. In fact, these individuals earn more than high school graduates without a trade certificate.[3] The returns from a trade certificate (versus dropping out of high school) are higher for men than for women, while the returns from university education are higher for women than for men – which may explain why more women and fewer men are currently attending university.

As we have seen, though, entry to the skilled trades for those without a high school diploma is not a panacea. More and more, the skilled trades require a solid base of knowledge that is gained through high school and college. Once somebody has attained a skilled trade, it is important for that person to stay current and to gain new skills as demand in the economy changes.

In a knowledge economy, it is almost certain that those without a base level of skills will be left behind. We are seeing that now. The public-policy imperative is to find ways to encourage (even coerce – as in Ontario, where the provincial government made school attendance compulsory to the age of eighteen in 2006) youth to complete their high school diploma. We need to make a concerted effort to strengthen apprenticeship programs, including creatively addressing the economic challenge of ensuring that the benefits and costs are borne by the same people. Currently, apprenticeship programs suffer from a free-rider problem. Employers who invest in apprenticeships are creating skills that other employers can benefit from.

More generally, we need to continue to explore creative pedagogical approaches for high school students who show little interest in staying in school. The Pathways to Education Program has proved to be an effective model for ensuring that young people from at-risk communities stay in school, graduate, and move on to post-secondary programs. The community-based program began in Toronto's Regent Park in 2001 and has since expanded to eleven neighbourhoods in four provinces.

The program provides academic tutoring, career mentoring, and financial assistance for transportation to and from school, and it helps to build stable relationships between young people, parents, and school staff. Results from the program are impressive.[4] For example, Pathways has reduced high school dropout rates by 70 per cent. It has resulted in a fourfold increase in the number of students going on to post-secondary education. We encourage community groups across Canada to explore ways they can help their at-risk youth complete high school and consider post-secondary paths.

Time and Child-Care Pressures Challenge Single Parents

The number of lone parents and children in lone-parent families has been increasing in recent years. As we have seen, families with lone parents have the worst economic outcomes – as defined by probability of being in the bottom two quintiles of income.

Lone-parent families are more likely to have incomes below LICO. Yet single parents have made the most progress in moving out of the bottom quintile, as welfare policies have responded to their challenges, and they have been more involved in the labour force. Participation rates of single mothers have risen faster than those for other Canadians. Their unemployment rate fell faster between 1995 and 2005 (it also increased fastest between 1990 and 1995). Single fathers are a small proportion of single parents and have not experienced the same trends in participation and unemployment. Still, lone parents trail all others in market income and after-tax, after-transfer income.[5]

Participation and employment results differ by level of education. Single mothers who are high school dropouts have a much lower attachment to the labour force than other Canadians – with lower participation rates and higher unemployment rates. Single mothers who are university graduates actually have slightly higher participation rates and about the same unemployment rates as other Canadian university graduates.

The key public-policy challenge is to create incentives for low-skilled single mothers that make it economically advantageous for them to find and keep employment. As we discussed elsewhere in this book, low-income Canadians face very high marginal effective tax rates as they move up the income ladder, to around the $20,000-mark.

A recent experiment by the Social Research and Demonstration Corporation, funded by Human Resources and Skills Development Canada (HRSDC), indicates that programs can be designed to encourage single mothers to work. The Self-Sufficiency Project, based heavily on incentives to make it economically advantageous for lone mothers to work,[6] initially delivered positive employment results. The experiment supplemented wages for single mothers who made the transition from welfare to work.

The supplement covered the difference between the actual wage and an annual benchmark of $37,500. Early results were encouraging, improving employment outcomes and reducing welfare receipts. However, the supplement was in effect for only three years. Once it ended, a significant percentage of the participants' employment fell and the long-term benefits did not match the three-year costs.

The key lesson learned is that incentives can succeed in helping single parents and other low-income people find work. But the incentives must persist for the benefits to last. The experiment lends support to the positive potential of the Working Income Tax Benefit.

Persons with Disabilities Have Difficulties Gaining Skills and Access to the Labour Market

Persons with disabilities made up approximately 7 per cent of our population in the 2006 census[7] and have an above-average risk of living in poverty. Since the incidence of disability increases with age, 47 per cent of those sixty-five and older have disabilities. This proportion of persons with disabilities is only expected to grow as our population ages.

Disabilities can take many forms. The Participation and Activity Limitation Survey (PALS) identifies ten different areas of disability: hearing, seeing, speech, mobility, agility, pain, learning, memory, developmental, and psychological. Among Canadians aged twenty-five to sixty-four, the disabled have lower educational attainment and participate less in the labour market than persons without disabilities. There is a gap of thirty-seven percentage points in the labour-force participation rate, with only 47 per cent of those with moderate, severe, or very severe disabilities participating in the labour force. Even when they are employed, they earn on average only 78 per cent of what a non-disabled person would earn.

The average level of highest educational attainment is also lower for this group. While 19 per cent of Canadians without a disability have not graduated from high school, this rises to 27 per cent for those with a disability. While 21 per cent of persons without a disability have a university degree, only 13 per cent of those with a disability do. A significant number of Canadians who had a disability during their educational years report that it affected their schooling and career choices.

The Martin Prosperity Institute assessment of the 2005 Accessibility for Ontarians with Disabilities Act (AODA)[8] estimated that increased participation by those with disabilities in our labour market could raise GDP per capita by up to $650; higher educational attainment could add another $200. Together, these two factors could close 9 per cent of Canada's prosperity gap with the United States.

AODA attempts to eliminate the barriers that the disabled face in everyday life. Examples of areas covered by the AODA include:

- building codes – creating new buildings that are designed from the ground up to be more accessible;
- public transportation – accessible vehicles and platforms, audio and visual aids, and so on;
- employment practices – formal recognition of the need for accommodation of employees with different limitations; and
- information and communication – accessible websites and media.

Clearly, the act works toward enabling more people to participate productively in society. This is especially important when more and more of us will depend on such measures in the future.

Unattached Individuals Forty-Five to Sixty-Four Are Growing in Number and Lagging Economically

The number of unattached individuals between ages forty-five and sixty-four is increasing at about twice the rate as that for all individuals in the age group (a 177 per cent increase between 1980 and 2006 versus a 86 per cent increase for all individuals aged forty-five to sixty-four). The data indicate a variety of reasons for being unattached – for example, marriage breakdown, widowhood, never been married. These people tend more than others in their age group to have disabilities.

The key economic factor affecting this group appears to be low labour-force participation. In 1980 unattached individuals forty-five to sixty-four had a participation rate equal to the age cohort as a whole. This has drifted lower over the past twenty years, so that in 2010 the gap in the participation rate was about seven percentage points. The group has experienced chronically higher unemployment rates (about two to three percentage points higher in unemployment). Consequently, its utilization rate has drifted lower. In general, this group tends to be less well educated.[9]

Recent Immigrants Are Not Participating in the 'Canadian Dream'

Recent immigrants' earnings have been falling behind other Canadians' earnings. But this is not a new phenomenon. Since 1985, results from the Census have shown immigrants' incomes trailing those of native-born Canadians, and this gap is widening. In the 2006 Census, immigrants to Canada within the past five years were 2.6 times as likely as the Canadian-born to have income below LICO. This ratio has worsened since 1980, when it stood at 1.4.[10] Researchers point to several factors that help explain this poor situation:[11]

- There are more immigrants now than in the past, and we no longer adjust immigration levels to differing levels of unemployment overall.
- While more recent immigrants are likely to have a university degree, they have skill levels below those of comparable Canadian-born graduates. Obviously, those less proficient in our official languages will have lower literacy skills, but even recent immigrants speaking English or French at home also had less-developed literacy skills. The gap is narrowest for numeracy skills and wider for literacy and problem-solving skills.
- The distribution of our recent immigrants' country of origin has changed over the past few decades. Traditional sources of our immigrants – the United States, northern and southern Europe, the Caribbean, Latin America, and southeast Asia – now account for a smaller share of immigrants to Canada. Other regions – eastern Europe, south, east, and west Asia, and Africa – now have a larger share. The cultural, language, educational, and discrimination hurdles for these newer immigrants are likely higher. It is also more difficult to assess the education and work experience that these immigrants bring to Canada.
- Immigrants are facing stiffer competition from the more highly educated Canadian-born. More Canadians have university education than in the past, and this reduces the educational advantage of immigrants. Should we be more selective in which immigrants we admit to Canada? In 1996 Australia instituted changes to its immigration policies to be more selective in its screening. Australian researcher Leslie Hawthorne studied the changes in economic outcomes for immigrants to Australia and found a marked improvement compared to Canada. Some argue that we should adopt the Australian approach and be more selective. Others counter that Canada shouldn't poach the most highly skilled from developing economies and should welcome immigrants irrespective of their skills and provide them with an opportunity to create a good life here.

For us, the key poverty-reduction approach for recent immigrants is greater investment in upgrading their skills to make them more applicable in a Canadian context. The federal and provincial governments have several initiatives underway.

Attachment to the Workforce Is the Key Challenge for Aboriginal People

As a group, Aboriginal people (on and off reserves) tend to participate in the labour force much less than other Canadians, and they have chronically higher unemployment.

Between 2000 and 2005, Aboriginal people increased their participation rate in the labour force from 70 to 73 per cent. Over the same period, the participation rate for non-Aboriginal people was unchanged at 80 per cent. So the participation gap narrowed slightly.

Unemployment rates for Aboriginal people fell from 17 per cent to 13 per cent, while non-Aboriginals experienced a decline from 6 per cent to 5 per cent. Consequently, the utilization rate – the percentage of adults who are working – increased for Aboriginal people over the 2000–5 period. Still, a sizable gap existed between them and non-Aboriginal people. While Aboriginal people are as likely to participate in the labour force as those in other risk groups, their unemployment rate is much higher.

A study by economist Michael Hatfield of HRSDC noted that off-reserve Aboriginal people outperformed the other risk groups in securing stable paid employment;[12] still, they did not perform as well as those outside the risk groups. Our analysis, which includes on-reserve and off-reserve Aboriginal people, does not detect this advantage versus other risk groups. However, it seems reasonable to conclude that on-reserve Aboriginal people are underperforming their off-reserve counterparts considerably.

In exploring their economic performance more closely, we find that Aboriginal people are also more likely to be part of other risk groups – particularly single parents, high school dropouts, and persons with disabilities.[13] Aboriginal people not in any other risk group achieve better economic performance than Aboriginal people who have these other risk factors. Nevertheless, they still trail the economic performance of Canadians not in these risk groups.

Aboriginal people who are in the workforce tend more to be in lower-paying occupations and less in higher-paying ones. While 35 per cent of all Canadian workers are in Richard Florida's creative class, only 22 per cent of Aboriginal people are. Aboriginal people underperform others in the same occupation. This is especially true of higher-paying occupations; for example, in nursing, Aboriginal people earn 25 per cent less than their non-Aboriginal counterparts, while as managers they earn less than half what non-Aboriginals earn.

Others have conducted more research into the social and economic challenges facing Aboriginal people. They conclude that our current policies are not successful in helping Aboriginals contribute to, and benefit from, our economic success.[14] According to recent research, the two most critical areas with respect to Aboriginal people's educational attainment are the transition from primary to secondary school and the much higher dropout rates and lower performance prevalent in on-reserve as opposed to off-reserve high schools.

We need creative, innovative strategies focused on Aboriginal people's unique circumstances. The status quo is unsatisfactory.

Prosperity Is Unequally Distributed

Nearly all would agree at a general level that the distribution of prosperity is an important issue for an economy. A high rate of inequality, in which too much of an economy's prosperity ends up in the hands of a few, is unsustainable.

Significant inequality means that certain individuals are not contributing to prosperity as much as they might, and so the economy is not realizing its full potential. Also, it often leads to political and social instability. At the other extreme, complete equality of economic outcomes has never been achieved. Nor is it desirable; achieving high levels of equality by heavy taxation of upper-income earners reduces incentives and encourages highly skilled people to move elsewhere. So, while most will agree that some degree of inequality is desirable, or at least inevitable, achieving consensus on the right distribution is difficult. In addition, measuring the rate of inequality is fraught with complexities.

Exhibit 47 **Higher inequality is not determined by higher average prosperity**

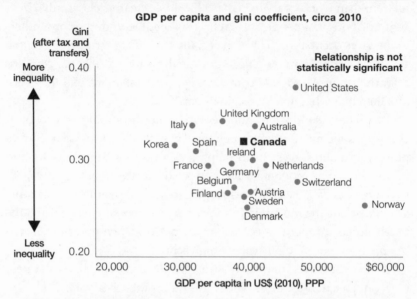

GDP per capita and gini coefficient, circa 2010

Note: The Gini coefficient measures the degree to which income or other resources or outcomes are shared across the population. A Gini of 1 means that everybody shares exactly equally. A Gini of 0 means that one person has everything. Ginis are adjusted for household size.
Source: Institute for Competitiveness & Prosperity analysis based on data from OECD (2011), *Society at a Glance 2011 – OECD Social Indicators.*

Among developed economies, inequality is not related to the level of average prosperity. When we plot GDP per capita against the inequality of market incomes (before government measures that reduce inequality through progressive taxation and transfer programs) and against inequality of disposable income (after taxes and transfers), we find no relationship. That is, more unequal economies like the United States, Canada, United Kingdom, and Australia are not necessarily more or less prosperous than more equal economies like Sweden, Denmark, the Netherlands, or Norway (Exhibit 47).

A major challenge with inequality is that it can become an intergenerational cycle that becomes even harder to break. If income is concentrated at the top and there are inadequate opportunities for children with disadvantaged backgrounds to receive the education they need to move out of poverty, an economy will not benefit from their contribution, will underperform, and will be stuck in a vicious circle of high inequality and low prosperity. Nobel Laureate James Heckman sets out the risks of illiteracy and low skills among children in lower-income families. These risks lead to reduced national productivity and prosperity for future generations.[15]

Currently, intergenerational income mobility is a strength for Canada. Statistics Canada researcher Miles Corak finds that only 20 per cent of the parental-earnings advantage in Canada is passed on to our children, a rate similar to that in Scandinavian countries. This compares favourably to countries like the United States, the United Kingdom, and France, where 40 to 50 per cent of the advantage is passed on.[16]

Since the 1980s, we have been witnessing higher levels of inequality in developed economies. Much of the research focus has been on U.K. and U.S. inequality, but most developed economies have experienced a similar trend. Several factors account for the emerging inequality:

- Relative wages paid to university graduates have increased sharply, demonstrating the increasing premium for education.
- Average wages for older workers have increased relative to those for younger workers and those with lower levels of education.
- Demand for workers with skills in computers and computerized equipment is higher than in the past.
- Employment has shifted away from unionized manufacturing jobs, which provided relatively high wages for less well-educated males, to lower-paying non-union jobs in other sectors.
- Growth in minimum wages has not kept pace with general wage growth.
- Expansion of international trade and offshoring has increased the pressure on low-skilled workers in developed economies.
- Compensation rewards have increased significantly for senior executives and other high earners – a winner-take-all phenomenon. Research by economists Emmanuel Saez and Michael Veall into

Canadian income-tax results during the 1985 to 2000 period, when inequality grew most, shows a dramatic increase in the proportion of personal income garnered by the top 10 per cent of tax filers – growing from 35 per cent in 1985 to 42 per cent in 2000. Of this seven-percentage-point increase, the top 1 per cent gained five percentage points, while the remaining 9 per cent gained only two percentage points.[17]

Economists continue to debate why inequality has risen over the past few decades. We conclude that developed economies are becoming more sophisticated and are valuing more advanced skills. As we showed earlier, jobs that require more analytical and social- intelligence skills pay better than those with lower-skill requirements. Over the past few decades, the income premium for a university degree has risen. We're also seeing that jobs that demand more physical skill pay less than those with low physical requirements. And, finally, the income ratio between those at the top of the income distribution to those in the middle and at the bottom has increased, while the ratio between the middle and lowest income earners hasn't changed much.[18]

Overall, we are seeing more inequality across developed economies, largely as a result of structural changes that are providing higher rewards to those with the particular skills in demand. These structural changes from technology and globalization are increasing prosperity and inequality simultaneously. Still, it is inaccurate to say that higher prosperity drives increases in inequality.

What Is the Linkage between Inequality and Poverty?

We conclude that reducing poverty should be the priority, not reducing inequality. Policies explicitly aimed at increasing equality will not necessarily improve the conditions affecting poverty; nor will they necessarily increase our economy's competitiveness and prosperity. But we can work to alleviate poverty directly. In fact, this will lead to higher prosperity through wider inclusion. Andrew Sharpe notes:

The two-way linkages between economic growth and inequality may set up situations where virtuous (or vicious) circles can be created. For example, strong economic growth generates additional tax revenues that can be redistributed to the poor, reducing inequality, enhancing their opportunities to get ahead, and stimulating further economic growth. This growth in turn produces more tax revenue. Equally, the adoption of policies that redistribute income can reduce inequality and create better opportunities for the poor. This in turn strengthens growth and generates tax revenues. *Good economic policymaking is the hunt for virtuous circles. Growth-equality linkages represent a fertile environment for such a hunt.'*[19]

We agree. And the best way to achieve this virtuous circle is to alleviate poverty among high-risk groups.

We need strategies that make real inroads into reducing poverty and increasing prosperity for as many Canadians as possible. We think that it is more important to focus on public policy that reduces poverty among these high-risk groups than to strive for greater equality by holding back opportunities for other Canadians. And, since each of these groups is excluded from Canada's prosperity for its own reasons, each requires its own tailored solution.

Innovative and highly focused public policies and programs must be established, with education being an important – if not, the most important – solution to reducing poverty. Innovative programs such as the Working Income Tax Benefit and wage insurance can provide encouragement for individuals in high-risk groups to find work, and, in this case, potentially foster job creation.

We should continue to strive for the best policy initiatives for helping people escape poverty. If we are not successful in assisting individuals in these groups to move out of poverty, we are hurting our future prosperity potential. We need the skills and capabilities of all Canadians to create economic success, and we cannot afford to ignore people in these high-risk groups. If Canada succeeds in realizing its full economic potential by pursuing focused and innovative solutions for addressing poverty, more Canadians will contribute to and participate in the rewards of enhanced prosperity.

13 Make Canada What It Can Be

Throughout this book we have been making recommendations to move Canada from what it is to what it can be – a truly innovative and prosperous country that sets the standard for the rest of the world. Some of our recommendations are to adopt best practices, but as much as possible we've set out innovations for our governments, businesses, and citizens. Canada has been innovative in many ways, and that's when we've done best.

Here are twelve specific recommendations.

Strengthen Our Determination to Close the Prosperity Gap

Telling Canadians that we need to perform better in areas of productivity, innovation, and competitiveness is a tough sell. This is the best place to live in the world, and we have a very competitive economy. That's because we're a job-creating machine for all Canadians who want to work, and we're blessed with plenty of natural resources that are in demand these days. But we're innovation laggards, and our long-term prosperity can't be taken for granted. There is certainly no burning platform that serves as a call to action. Nevertheless, we urge our political and business leaders to raise the issue with Canadians and to look earnestly for policies and strategies that help close the prosperity gap.

Ensure That Our Public Policy Balances Spending on Current Prosperity and Investing in Future Prosperity

Canadians love their health-care system and want it to be there for them and their loved ones. So do we. But it's crowding out investments we need to be making for the future prosperity that will ensure the continuance of our health-care system. When choices between spending on health care and education had to be made over the past three decades, our governments chose the former. No doubt that's where the votes were. We need to be open to serious reforms in health care, so that its spending growth – and demographics are putting great pressure on spending – is kept to the absolute minimum. As governments fight the deficits created during the recent recession, they need to ensure that investments in future prosperity like education are a priority. We're also open to the suggestion that it would be beneficial to seriously review how we spend our education dollars. In all our priorities and programs, we must spend wisely.

Increase Aspirations for and Access to Post-Secondary Education

If there's one anti-poverty policy that applies almost everywhere, it's greater educational attainment. It's a tragedy for someone to leave high school without a diploma, and there are still too many who do. We need to ensure that we do everything we can to cajole and support our children to get through high school – at the very least. At the same time, we need to raise the aspirations of our young people to go as far as they can in post- secondary education. Financial assistance can help, but the real barriers are attitudinal on the part of parents and children.

Shift the Balance in Our Public Policy from Invention to Innovation

Canada's public policies focus on inventing new things and then hoping our scientists can 'commercialize' them. Invention is very important for our future, but innovation in our products, services, and processes will drive competitiveness and prosperity for Canadians. Let's focus our policies on pulling more ideas and research in support of innovation rather than hoping that R&D spending by itself will drive innovation.

Teach Innovation to Our Children

Thirty years ago, we didn't teach computer skills to our children in school; now we do. That's because the computer has become ubiquitous, and many jobs require some level of computer skills. As developing countries like Brazil, India, and China move toward their innovation tipping points, we are heading to a future where innovation will matter as it never did before. We can get well and truly ahead of this if our future workers and managers are the most skilled in innovation in the world. Let's decide to teach innovation in our primary and secondary schools. We have some ideas on what that teaching would entail – but there's much more we can learn and teach.

Build Our Management Capabilities

Strong management capabilities are necessary conditions for innovation – in developing breakthrough business strategies and in day-to-day operations. Unfortunately, our management cadre could be stronger. We know they're not as well educated, regardless of discipline, as they should and could be, and we know that our post-secondary education system produces fewer business graduates than that of the United States. Public policy and dollars have galvanized the need for scientists and engineers in the past. The evidence shows that we need a similar effort in management. Our business leaders have to look critically at the management skills in their organizations, and our university administrators have to ensure that their offerings match student demand for business education.

Continue to Lower Taxes on Business Investment

Our federal government and most of our provincial governments have implemented smart tax policies that are making Canada one of the best places for business investments. But some of our provinces still have antiquated tax systems that discourage business investment. Ontario's recent shift from a retail sales tax to a value-added harmonized sales tax and its reduction of corporate income tax rates were an important breakthrough for the province and the country. It's too bad that the British Columbia voters turned their back on similar measures, and that other provinces like Manitoba, Saskatchewan, and Prince Edward Island have not taken up reform. We encourage governments in these provinces to finish the job and make Canada a low-tax jurisdiction everywhere.

Pursue True Tax-Policy Innovation

We're pleased with the tax-policy changes that have been implemented on the business front. These have helped us catch up with other developed economies. But we urge Canadians to be true innovators in tax policy. We've been making good progress in moving the system away from taxing investment and income to taxing consumption. Let's go further and explore ideas that are already on the table. Let's seriously consider a carbon tax. And let's put our minds to solving the seemingly intractable problem of high marginal effective tax rates for low-income Canadians trying to move up the income ladder.

Adopt Targeted Anti-Poverty Policies

The incidence of poverty is highly focused among specific groups in Canada. The challenges faced by those without a high school diploma are different from those of our recent immigrants or single parents. We need to redouble our efforts for targeted policies. For us, the inequality debate is less important. We care deeply about people who have the least income. By helping them help themselves, we can reduce poverty and inequality at the same time.

Adopt Reciprocity as Our Guiding Principle for Foreign Direct Investment

The net-benefit test for evaluating foreign takeovers is too vague and is open to political, not economic, evaluations. In trade policy, multilateral and bilateral deals are based on reciprocity. The parties agree to open their markets to each other with consistent rules applying to all sides. Explicit exceptions are still possible. We should apply this to foreign takeovers, so that our governments will allow takeovers by companies from countries whose own firms can be acquired by Canadian ones.

Expand International Trade

Canada has a relatively small population and we have to work at expanding our markets and our supply base. Similarly, we can't rely on our domestic economy to provide the support and pressure necessary for innovation. More than many other countries, Canada needs to trade internationally. Our federal government has shown an eagerness to negotiate trade deals. We applaud these efforts and urge ongoing focus on fewer but bigger deals.

Innovate in Venture Funding

It is important that our entrepreneurial start-ups benefit from enough high-quality venture funding. Here, our past efforts in Canada have failed with respect both to quantity and to quality. We conclude that trying to replicate the U.S. venture-capital model in Canada will not meet our needs. This model is broken and is not likely coming back. We should lead the rest of the world in developing new models. Lean financing tends to be smaller in scope and is based on a more hands-on approach than what we have seen in Canada to date. Perhaps there are ways that our governments can help get the lean-financing models working in Canada.

Implementing these recommendations may not be easy or quick. But that is no reason not to start on the path that will lead to Canada's future prosperity. Not doing so will place the well-being of all Canadians at risk in the globalizing world in which we now live.

EPILOGUE

Let's look ahead to 2025 and imagine two futures – one based on our current trajectory, 'what Canada is' – and one based on a retuned Canada, 'what Canada can be.'

For Michael and Maria, the major difference between the two futures is our health-care system. They'll be retiring around 2025 and living better than most other retirees, with two solid employer-funded retirement plans to support them. They may decide to keep working in their current jobs or different jobs to keep active – but it's not likely they'll be doing it for the money. But they will be older, and aging will start to show. They can expect more ailments and doctors' visits.

In the Canada-as-it-is trajectory, they'll be increasingly concerned about whether our governments can afford the health-care system that we enjoy now. All federal and provincial finance ministers will find it more and more difficult to find resources to meet the ever more costly health-care system. That's because economic output has not grown as fast as it could have – and we risk falling behind other countries. Hence, tax revenues are not as robust as they used to be, and increasing tax rates would only hurt economic output further.

In the Canada-as-it-can-be trajectory, higher productivity and innovation will have increased our economic output even as the workforce shrinks through the impact of demographics. This economic success story in Canada will mean that governments have the tax revenues to support the growing demands of our public health-care system. Michael and Maria won't be worrying so much about whether or not the public system will be there for them. Nor will their children and their families.

Sandra's prospects will be much different depending on which path Canada takes. Like other single mothers with only a high school diploma, she'll find that she lacks the skills and time to advance in the job market. She can also expect ongoing barriers to moving up the income ladder because of the high Marginal Effective Tax Rates at her income level. And she'll find it difficult to get that university degree.

But if Canada adopts innovative social policies that are focused on the specific challenges of those at risk, including single mothers, Sandra will have a better chance of advancing in her work or getting a degree or both. Policy changes require fixing the high METRs for low-income Canadians, providing an enhanced and better-designed Working Income Tax Benefit, and implementing creative policies to help increase access to post-secondary education. And, needless to say, her son will have an even better chance of breaking out of the cycle of poverty that Sandra may be starting.

Kevin can expect a decently rewarding career in financial services even if Canada stays on its current trajectory. But his current firm may find it tougher and tougher to compete globally. If our investment banks continue to be me-too competitors, they'll be marginal players in Canadian deals and won't participate in deals happening outside Canada. Kevin's firm may get bought out by an offshore competitor; or he could get laid off as the volume of deals for him to work on dries up. He may be attracted to move to the United States or even China or India as they move toward the innovation tipping point. That would be a loss to the Schmidt family and to Canada.

But if Canada's innovation policies and its competitive intensity are made more intelligent, Kevin's firm might be forced to step up its performance. Its partners would realize that just competing for a small share of available Canadian deals was a losing strategy. Instead, like some Canadian manufacturers who stepped up to the challenges and opportunities of U.S.-Canada free trade, they would develop their small portfolio of foreign business more aggressively and challenge themselves to be global leaders in a segment of the investment-banking business. Kevin's earnings would be on a steeper trajectory, but, perhaps more important, he would be working on some of the most interesting and challenging deals in the world. Moving abroad would be the furthest thing from his mind – unless it was to set up a branch for his firm in China or India. If he did move, the Schmidts would miss him, but he would likely return to head office after his stint abroad.

How would Louise, who is just starting her post-secondary education, fare under the two different futures? More than likely, she'll get her undergraduate degree and go into the workforce. She'll do well, since a bachelor's degree is a financially rewarding investment. Yet, whatever job in whatever industry she chooses, she'll probably earn less than her counterparts in the United States.

But if Canada becomes what it can be, she may be more likely to pursue a graduate degree in her chosen field. Our increasingly sophisticated firms will find that they need the added skills and capabilities that come from a master's degree and pay her more than what she would have earned in a Canada-as-it-is future. Like Kevin, she'll have a better chance of working for a Canadian firm that is a global leader in its industry. And if she chooses a career in the sciences, she'll find that more of her work leads to real innovation.

We're confident that Canada will still be the best place to live in the year 2025. But there are no guarantees, and we can't take for granted that Canada will continue to be an economic leader. What we're proposing are policies that improve our odds of achieving our full economic potential.

ACKNOWLEDGMENTS

This book had its beginnings back in 2001 when Ontario Premier Mike Harris asked Roger Martin to lead a task force to measure and monitor Ontario's economic progress and to make recommendations for its long-term success. Other initiatives like this typically mean a flurry of consultation and work culminating in a big report with lots of press coverage in the ensuing forty-eight hours. And then nothing.

But the premier and his colleagues at the Ministry of Economic Development and Trade wanted something different. So the Task Force on Competitiveness, Productivity and Economic Progress developed a modus operandi that gave it wide latitude to investigate the areas we thought important and to report directly to the public, not to a government group or a cabinet committee. The government provided funds for an institute to carry out the economic research in support of the Task Force's work – the Institute for Competitiveness & Prosperity. Jim Milway has been its executive director for most of its life.

We did not have a specific deadline, but the government agreed to provide funding for three years; this agreement could be renewed or ended at any time with perfunctory notice from the province. We determined to let the research take us where it did and to report honestly and directly what we concluded.

We're proud to say that, ten years and two premiers later, we're still in business. We have produced ten Annual Reports for Ontario, fifteen Working Papers on topics ranging from industry clusters to taxation, and from trade to poverty and inequality. Along the way we were advised to broaden our horizons from Ontario to Canada, and to this end we presented nine Reports on Canada. We've had an influence on economic policy provincially and nationally – in areas of innovation, post-secondary education, anti-poverty, and venture-capital policy.

This book is our tenth annual 'report' on Canada's economic progress and outlook. It's an attempt to pull together and synthesize themes from the work of the Task Force and the Institute into a coherent whole that urges Canadians to aspire to greater economic progress – to a level we think is entirely achievable.

It is no exaggeration to say that this book would not have been possible without the support of successive provincial governments led by Mike Harris, Ernie Eves, and Dalton McGuinty and economic development ministers Bob Runciman, Jim Flaherty, Joe Cordiano, Sandra Pupatello, Michael Bryant, and Brad Duguid. All of them gave us the moral support to call things as we saw them – even when it made their political lives a little uncomfortable. On a day-to-day basis, we have a great working relationship with Ministry of Economic Development and Innovation staff led by current Deputy Minster Wendy Tillman and Assistant Deputy Minister (ADM) Maurice Bitran. For most of our ten years, we worked with former ADM Bob Seguin. Bob was there at the creation and was a steady and wise liaison between us and the government.

Our current and past Task Force members included some of the ablest business people and academics in Canada – John Armstrong, Jim Balsillie, Tim Dattells, Lisa de Wilde, David Folk, Suzanne Fortier, Michael Gourley, Gord Homer, Tom Jenkins, Jacques Lamarre, Jacques Ménard, Mark Mullins, William Orovan, David Keddie, Tim Penner, Belinda Stronach, and Dan Trefler. In addition to giving us guidance on our research agenda and conclusions, all of them have been generous with personal time on specific issues in their areas of expertise.

At the outset, we determined that the Institute ought to be constituted as an incorporated company with its own board of directors. Our board members – Michael Akkawi, Chris Riddle, who ably launched the

Institute as its first executive director, Suzanne Spragge, and Martha Tory – have guided us well since the Institute's inception, and we value their contributions over the years.

Also present at the creation was our esteemed colleague Michael Porter at the Harvard Business School's Institute for Strategy and Competitiveness. Michael, along with Christian Ketels and Rich Bryden, helped us in our early days and the three of them still do so now with data and advice on clustered industries – one of the areas we have concentrated on in our own work.

We're fortunate to have a smart and generous group of colleagues at the Rotman School and the University of Toronto whom we can call on for advice or knowledge. Richard Florida and Kevin Stolarick, at our sister organization, the Martin Prosperity Institute, have been thought partners in much of our work, and you'll see their fingerprints throughout the book. Dan Trefler is a Task Force member but also a day-to-day friend and co-conspirator in a lot of our work. We thank also Ajay Agrawal, Michelle Alexopoulos, Don Brean, Morley Gunderson, Michael Hare, Walid Hejazi, Jack Mintz, Peter Pauly, and David Soberman for help along the way – giving us advice or speaking at our events. Steve Arenburg, Jack Thompson, and Ken McGuffin were always generous with their time to help us reach out to media and plan events.

From Day 1, we thought it really important to communicate our findings and messages in understandable prose and compelling graphics. We've had fantastic partners. Diane Nelles has helped us structure our work – pulling together the research strands into coherent storylines and relentlessly pruning the material that we loved but wasn't that interesting to a normal person. She ably helped us with the big picture and the minutiae. Bob Hambly and Barb Woolley, with their colleagues at Hambly & Woolley, especially Gord Woolley, contributed mightily over the years with design concepts and charts that helped communicate clearly. Thanks to Andrew Ryther who prepared most of the exhibits in this book.

The heavy lifting for the book was carried out by successive groups of our small bands of researchers – young, smart people whom we challenged with research hypotheses to be tested and who challenged us with the facts and better hypotheses. They're hard-working young people who give us great confidence that Canada's future is secure. We're proud to be associated with them. Our current group – Tamer Azer, Colin Bradley, Satyajit (Sunny) Dutt, Shabnam Mohsenzadeh, Melissa Pogue, and Rebecca Sun – did a lot of original research for this book and updated facts and figures. They were assisted greatly by researchers who recently left for graduate school – Katherine Chan, Anam Kidwai, Lloyd Martin, and Aaron Meyer. They successfully met the standards set by our previous researchers whose work contributed significantly to this book – Riaz Ahmed, Mary Albino, Lance Bialas, Jordan Brennan, Courtney Chiu, Nimira Dharamshi, Chris Hilborn, Roy Hrab, Alberto Isgut, Sam Ladner, Omar Madhany, Jerome McGrath, Mary Monaghan, Usman Naeem, Sana Nisar, Zoe Oldman, Claurelle Poole, Adrienne Ross, Stephen Rouatt, Daniela Scur, Robert Sinclair, Hanan Stefan, Jennifer Stewart, Sunny Sun, Charlotte Warren, Ying Wang, and Melody Yiu.

It's been great working with the University of Toronto Press, especially editor Jennifer DiDomenico. We benefited greatly from her advice and guidance through this project.

From Roger, a personal note of thanks to his wife, Sandra Blevins, and his children, Lloyd and Daniel. One of the joys of his life to date was working with Lloyd during his years as a researcher at the Institute for Competitiveness & Prosperity.

From Jim, a personal note of thanks to his wife, Sheila – his biggest fan, proudest supporter, and love of his life – and their children, Tom, Michael, Joan, Dan, and Peter; each one of them was called on during crunch times to gather data on global leaders, CEO biographies, and economic trivia.

This book has been written by two proud Canadians. Through the book, we point to the strengths of this great country and its citizens. From time to time, we're critical. But it's criticism coming from friends. Canada is the best place in the world to live, work, and play. We want to keep it that way – and do even better.

NOTES

1 What Are Competitiveness and Prosperity?

1 Institute for Competitiveness & Prosperity (Toronto), Working Paper 14, *Trade, innovation, and prosperity*, September 2010.
2 Paul Krugman, 'Competitiveness: A Dangerous Obsession,' *Foreign Affairs*, 73, no. 2 (1994): 28–44, and 'The Competition Myth,' *New York Times*, 24 January 2011, A27.
3 Michael Porter, *The Competitive Advantage of Nations* (New York: Free Press 1998), 6–8.
4 Centre for the Study of Living Standards (Ottawa), *Explaining Geographical Variation in Happiness in Canada*, November 2010.
5 GDP producing-power parity (PPP) extrapolated using GDP implicit chain price index. PPP base year taken from John R. Baldwin, Wulong Gu, and Beiling Yan, 'Relative Multifactor Productivity Levels in Canada and the United States: A Sectoral Analysis,' Statistics Canada, Catalogue no. 15–206–X–no. 019, 2008, 28. The Canada-US PPP for 2009 is 1.178 and for 2010 it is 1.203.
6 Canadian survey results as presented by the Innovative Research Group at the release of the Institute for Competitiveness & Prosperity's *Report on Canada 2008*. Available online at http://www.competeprosper.ca/images/uploads/ICP_presentation_20070308_Lyle.pdf.
7 Institute for Competitiveness & Prosperity, *Prosperity, inequality, and poverty*, September 2007, 25–7.
8 Leandro Prados de la Escosura and Isabel Sanz-Villarroya, 'Contract Enforcement, Capital Accumulation, and Argentina's Long-Run Decline,' *Cliometrica*, 3, no. 1 (2009).

2 How Much Are We Working for Prosperity?

1 Calculated as 1 – [67.0(U.S.)/69.4(Canada)] = 3.5 per cent.
2 Robin Banerjee and William Robson, *Faster, Younger, Richer?*, C.D. Howe Institute *Commentary*, no. 291 (2009).
3 Institute for Competitiveness & Prosperity, *Agenda for Canada's Prosperity*, Report on Canada 2007, 20.
4 Institute for Competitiveness & Prosperity, *Time on the job: Intensity and Ontario's prosperity gap*, Working Paper 9, September 2006, 21.
5 What we call the 'utilization' rate – the percentage of the working-age population who are employed – is typically referred to as the 'employment' rate by economists. We use the term 'employment' as the percentage of people who are in the labour force with jobs. This is 1 *minus* the unemployment rate.
6 Using results comparable to U.S. methods of calculation.
7 Using U.S. definitions. Canadian numbers reported in the press are different.
8 Institute for Competitiveness & Prosperity, *Time on the Job*, 31.

3 How Much Value Are We Creating When We Are Working?

1 Daniel Trefler, 'The Long and Short of the Canada-U.S. Free Trade Agreement,' *American Economic Review*, 94 (2004): 870–89; and Alla Lileeva and Daniel Trefler, 'Improved Access to Foreign Markets Raises Plant-Level Productivity ... for Some Plants,' *Quarterly Journal of Economics*, 125, no. 3 (2010): 877–921.
2 S.J. Prais, *Productivity, Education and Training: An International Perspective* (Cambridge: Cambridge University Press 1993), 54–7.
3 Federal Reserve Bank of Dallas, *Annual Report, 2003*.
4 Michael Porter, 'Building the Microeconomic Foundations of Prosperity: Findings from the Business Competitiveness Index,' *The Global Competitiveness Report 2003–2004*, World Economic Forum (2003), 31.

4 How Does Where We Live and Work Matter?

1 Richard Florida, *Who's Your City?* (New York: Basic Books 2008), 48.
2 Ibid., 19.
3 Meric Gertler. 'Economy and Society in Canada: Flows of People, Capital, and Ideas,' *Isuma: Canadian Journal of Policy Research*, 2, no. 3 (2001): 128.
4 Richard Florida, Charlotta Mellander, and Tim Gulden, 'Global Metropolis:

The Role of Cities and Metropolitan Areas in the Global Economy,' Martin Prosperity Institute Working Paper (2009), 10.

5 Richard Florida, Charlotta Mellander, and Tim Gulden, 'The Rise of the Mega Region,' *Cambridge Journal of Regions, Economy and Society*, 1, no. 3 (2008): 460.

6 Pierre-Philippe Combes et al., 'The Productivity Advantages of Large Cities: Distinguishing Agglomeration from Firm Selection,' CEPR Discussion Paper No. DP7191 (2009), 1.

7 Edward Glaeser, 'Why Humanity Loves and Needs Cities,' *New York Times*, 13 April 2010, http://www.economix.blogs.nytimes.com/2010/04/13/why-humanity-loves-and-needs-cities.

8 Gerald Carlino et al., 'Urban Density and the Rate of Invention,' *Journal of Urban Economics*, 61, no. 3 (2007): 389–419.

9 Glaeser, 'Why Humanity Loves and Needs Cities.'

10 Jane Jacobs, *The Economy of Cities* (New York: Random House 1969).

11 Richard Florida, *Technology and Tolerance: The Importance of Diversity to High-Technology Growth* (Washington, D.C.: Brookings Institution, Center on Urban and Metropolitan Policy, 2001).

12 David A. Wolfe and Allison Bramwell, 'Innovation, Creativity and Governance: Social Dynamics of Economic Performance in City Regions,' *Innovation: Management, Policy & Practice*, 10 (2008): 170–82.

13 Edward Glaeser and David Mare, 'Cities and Skills,' *Journal of Labor Economics*, 19, no. 2 (2001): 316–42.

14 Edward Glaeser and Matthew Resseger, 'The Complementarity between Cities and Skill,' *Journal of Regional Science*, 50, no. 1 (2009): 221–44.

15 Adam Jaffe et al., 'Geographic Localization of Knowledge Spillovers as Evidenced by Patent Citations,' *Quarterly Journal of Economics*, 108, no. 3 (1993).

16 The term 'social capital' was first used by Lyda Hanifan in 'The Rural School Community Center,' *Annals of the American Academy of Political and Social Science*, 67 (1916): 130–8.

17 After adjusting Canadian CMA definitions to US MSA definitions and adding ten smaller areas to the thirty-four official CMAs. See Statistics Canada, 'Defining and Measuring Metropolitan Areas: A Comparison between Canada and the United States,' Catalogue no. 92F0138M – No. 2008002 (2008).

18 Alfred Marshall, *Industry and Trade: A Study of Industrial Technique and Business Organization, and of Their Influences on the Conditions of Various Classes and Nations* (London: Macmillan 1919), 187.

19 Robert Lucas, Jr, 'On the Mechanics of Economic Development,' *Journal of Monetary Economics*, 22, no. 1 (1988): 3–42.

20 'Q&A with Michael Porter,' *Business Week*, 21 August 2006.
21 Jane Lin, 'Trends in Employment and Wages, 2002 to 2007,' Statistics Canada, *Perspectives*, Catalogue no. 75–001–X (2008).
22 Federal Reserve Bank of Dallas, *Annual Report, 2007*, 7–8.

5 How Do We Compete?

1 We have netted out the effects of other factors – Canada's lower urbaniza-tion, our under-investment in capital, and our lower educational attain-ment – in this calculation.
2 The research into attitudes we are referring to here was undertaken by the Institute for Competitiveness & Prosperity among the Ontario public, busi-ness people, and business leaders versus their counterparts in the large U.S. peer states. See the Institute's Working Paper 4, *Striking similarities: Attitudes and Ontario's prosperity gap*, September 2003.
3 Expert Panel on Business Innovation (Ottawa), *Innovation and Business Strategy: Why Canada Falls Short*, Council of Canadian Academies, 2009, 167 and 174.
4 Institute for Competitiveness & Prosperity, *Setting our sights on Canada's 2020 prosperity agenda*, Report on Canada 2008, April 2008, 34–5.
5 Deloitte Canada, *The Future of Productivity*, http://www.deloitte.com/assets/Dcom-Canada/Local%20Assets/Documents/Consulting/ca_en_productivity_complete_150611.pdf, 10–15.
6 See, for example, our 2007 research paper, *Assessing Toronto's Financial Services Cluster*, http://www.competeprosper.ca/images/uploads/FSstudy_June07.pdf.
7 See, for example, our 2004 research paper, *Assessing the Strength of Toron-to's Biopharmaceutical Cluster*, http://www.competeprosper.ca/images/uploads/biopharmaCluster.pdf.

6 How Do We Invest?

1 See Richard Dobbs, Andrew Grant, and Jonathan Woetzel, 'Unleashing the Chinese Consumer,' *Newsweek International*, 5 September 2009, for a review of the challenges facing the Chinese government as it attempts to change course from its priority on investment and industrialization while crowd-ing out consumers.
2 For a summary of the research on the economic benefits of investment in post-secondary education, see Institute for Competitiveness & Prosperity, *Canada's innovation imperative*, Report on Canada 2011, June 2011, 34–6.

3 Richard Florida, *Technology and Tolerance: The Importance of Diversity to High Technology Growth* (Washington, D.C.: Brookings Institution, Center on Urban and Metropolitan Policy, 2001).

4 Task Force on Competitiveness, Productivity and Economic Progress, 8th Annual Report, *Navigating through the recovery*, November 2009, 43–5.

5 In 2010 Canada's debt as a percentage of GDP was 84 per cent, while in the United States it was 94 per cent.

6 Bradford De Long and Lawrence Summers, 'Equipment Investment and Economic Growth: How Strong Is the Nexus?' *Brookings Papers on Economic Activity, Vol. 2* (Washington, D.C.: Brookings Institution 1992).

7 Andrew Sharpe, 'Unbundling Canada's Weak Productivity Performance: The Way Forward' (Ottawa: Centre for the Study of Living Standards 2010).

8 Xavier Sala-i Martin, 'I Just Ran Four Million Regressions,' *American Economic Review*, 87, no. 2 (1997): 178–83.

9 Pierre Fortin, 'The Canadian Standard of Living: Is There a Way Up?,' C.D. Howe Institute Benefactor's Lecture, 1999.

10 For our estimate, we assumed that higher growth in this investment would translate directly into higher growth in GDP.

7 Tax Smarter for Prosperity

1 For a summary of the research on the impact of lower taxes on business investment, see Task Force on Competitiveness, Productivity and Economic Progress, 7th Annual Report, *Leaning into the wind*, November 2008, 39–41.

2 Bev Dahlby and Egrete Ferede, 'What Does It Cost Society to Raise a Dollar of Revenue?,' C.D. Howe Institute *Commentary*, no. 324 (2011).

3 Jim Stanford, *Having Their Cake and Eating It Too* (Ottawa: Canadian Centre for Policy Alternatives 2011).

4 Michael Smart and Richard Bird, 'The Impact on Investment of Replacing a Retail Sales Tax with a Value-Added Tax: Evidence from Canadian Experience,' *National Tax Journal*, 62, no. 4 (2009).

5 TD Economics, 'The Impact of a Sales Tax Harmonization in Canada and B.C. on Canadian Inflation,' 18 September 2009.

6 Michael Smart, 'The Impact of Sales Tax Reform on Ontario Consumers: A First Look at the Evidence,' *SPP Research Papers*, School of Public Policy, University of Calgary (2011).

7 Jonathan Kesselman, 'Consumer Impacts of BC's Harmonized Sales Tax,' School of Public Policy, Simon Fraser University (2011).

8 Jack Mintz, 'Ontario's Bold Move to Create Jobs and Growth,' *SPP Communiqés*, School of Public Policy, University of Calgary (2009).
9 Jack Mintz, 'British Columbia's Harmonized Sales Tax: A Giant Leap in the Province's Competitiveness,' *SPP Briefing Papers*, School of Public Policy, University of Calgary (2010).
10 Institute for Competitiveness & Prosperity and Open Policy Ontario, *Time for a "Made in Ontario" Working Income Tax Benefit*, September 2009, 12.
11 This is the combined effect of federal and provincial personal income tax rates and brackets as well as deductions.
12 See Ross Finnie, 'The Dynamics of Poverty in Canada,' C.D. Howe Institute *Commentary*, no. 145 (2000); Morley Gunderson and Michael Trebilcock, 'Managing Labour Market Risk in the New World of Work,' Research Paper No. 10, Panel on the Role of Government in Ontario, 2003; Morley Gunderson, 'Active Labour Market Adjustment Policies: What We Know and Don't Know,' Research Paper No. 33, Panel on the Role of Government in Ontario, 2003; Michael J. Trebilcock, Ronald Daniels, Andrew J. Green, and Roy Hrab, 'Creating a Human Capital Society for Ontario,' Staff Report, Panel on the Role of Government in Ontario, 2004, 73–8.
13 Alexandre Laurin and Finn Poschmann, 'What's My METR? Marginal Effective Tax Rates Are Down – But Not for Everyone: The Ontario Case,' CD Howe *e-brief*, 4.
14 Finn Poschmann, 'Marginal and Average Effective Tax Burdens in Ontario,' July 2004, http://www.competeprosper.ca/images/uploads/FinnPoschmann_290305.pdf, 5.
15 Robert Frank, 'Just What This Downturn Demands: A Consumption Tax,' *New York Times*, 9 November 2008, BU8.
16 Jan Carr, 'A Rational Framework for Electricity Policy,' *Journal of Policy Engagement*, 2, no. 2 (2010).

8 Make Public Policy on Innovation More Innovative

1 William Buxton, 'Innovation vs. Invention,' *Rotman Magazine*, fall 2005, 52.
2 Steve Blank and Eric Ries, 'The Lean Startup – Low Burn by Design not Crisis,' http//www.slideshare.net/venturehacks/the-lean-startup-2.
3 Steve Lohr, 'The Rise of the Fleet-Footed Startup,' *New York Times*, 25 April 2010, BU5.

9 Strengthen Management Talent

1 Institute for Competitiveness & Prosperity, Working Paper 12, *Management matters*, March 2009, 14.

2 The Strategic Counsel, *Assessing the Experience of Successful Innovative Firms in Ontario*, September 2004, http://www.competeprosper.ca/images/uploads/InnovationInterviewStudyRep.pdf.

3 A study coordinated by Institute for Competitiveness & Prosperity and conducted by the Ontario Ministry of Economic Development and Trade. Institute for Competitiveness & Prosperity, Working Paper 12, *Management Matters*, 15.

4 She successfully developed this technique earlier as a measure of technological innovation, and she concludes that adapting it to management gives a good proxy for the diffusion of advanced management techniques across the economy.

5 Michelle Alexopoulos and Trevor Tombe, 'Management Matters,' forthcoming in *Journal of Monetary Economics* (2012).

6 Professor Nick Bloom of Stanford University and the Centre for Economic Performance at the London School of Economics has developed an interview method for evaluating management at manufacturing locations. The quality of management, as captured by his measures, correlates well with firm and industry productivity.

10 Bulk Up, Not Hollow Out

1 Canada's global leaders are defined as:

- a public or private Canadian-controlled company on *Report on Business Top 1000* or *Financial Post 500* lists;
- with revenues exceeding $100 million; and
- ranked as one of five largest by revenue globally in a specific market segment.

In some cases where global competition is precluded (for example, rail service and CN Rail), we used North America; in other cases, revenue was not the factor used (for example, we used market capitalization for Manulife).

2 Identified by Diane Francis in her book *Who Owns Canada Now: Old Money, New Money, and the Future of Canadian Business* (Toronto: HarperCollins 2008).

3 Ian Austen, 'Canada Wonders Why It's the Bought and Not the Buyer,' *New York Times*, 24 October 2006.

4 As identified by Mel Hurtig in *The Truth about Canada* (Toronto: Douglas Gibson Books 2008) and supplemented by our own research.

11 Become a True Trading Nation

1 See, for example, Robert Whaples, 'Do Economists Agree on Anything?

Yes!' *The Economists' Voice*, 3, no. 9, who found that 87.5 per cent of the members of the American Economic Association (AEA) agreed that 'the US should eliminate remaining tariffs and other barriers in trade.' Or Dan Fuller and Doris Geide-Stevenson, 'Consensus on Economic Issues: A Survey of Republicans, Democrats and Economists,' *Economic Journal*, 33, no. 1 (2007), who found that, in 2000, 72 per cent of AEA members agreed that 'tariffs and import quotas usually reduce the general welfare of society'; 21 per cent agreed, but with some provisos; and only 6 per cent disagreed.

2 Daniel Griswold, 'Obama's Protectionist Policies Hurting Low-Income Americans,' *Washington Times*, 29 September 2009.

3 Jeff Rubin, *Why Your World Is about to Get a Whole Lot Smaller* (Toronto: Random House Canada 2009).

4 Harold L. Sirkin, Michael Zinser, and Doug Hohner, *Made in America, Again: Why Manufacturing Will Return to the US* (Boston Consulting Group 2011), http://www.bcg.com/documents/file84471.pdf.

5 Kalina Manova, 'Credit Constraints and the Adjustment to Trade Reform,' in G. Porto, ed., *The Cost of Adjustment to Trade Reform*, World Bank Trade and Development Series (2010).

6 See Daniel Trefler, 'The Long and Short of the Canada-U.S. Free Trade Agreement,' *American Economic Review*, 94 (2004): 870–89; Alla Lileeva and Daniel Trefler, 'Improved Access to Foreign Markets Raises Plant-Level Productivity ... for Some Plants,' *Quarterly Journal of Economics*, 125, no. 3 (2010): 877–921; John Baldwin, Richard E. Caves, and Wulong Gu, 'Responses to Trade Liberalization: Changes in Product Diversification in Foreign and Domestic Controlled Plants,' in Lorraine Eden and Wendy Dobson, eds., *Governance, Multinationals and Growth* (Cheltenham, U.K.: Edward Elgar 2005), 209–46; and John Baldwin and Wulong Gu, 'Participation in Export Markets and Productivity Performance in Canadian Manufacturing,' *Canadian Journal of Economics*, 36 (2003): 634–57.

7 Philippe Aghion and Peter Howitt, *The Economics of Growth* (Cambridge, Mass.: MIT Press 2009).

8 The term 'tipping point' was popularized by Malcolm Gladwell, but Dan Trefler coined the phrase 'innovation tipping point' and the idea that developing economies reach this point as their institutions, businesses, and consumers become more sophisticated.

9 Daniel Trefler, 'Canadian Policy Responses to Offshore Outsourcing,' summary of the conference on 'Offshore Outsourcing: Capitalizing on Lessons Learned,' Rotman School of Management, University of Toronto, 26–27 October 2006.

10 Rubin, *Why Your World Is about to Get a Whole Lot Smaller*.

11 Trefler, 'Canadian Policy Responses to Offshore Outsourcing.'
12 Ibid.

12 Focus on Poverty, Not Inequality

1 For more information on the Gini coefficient and LICO and for a discussion of other measures of inequality and poverty, see Institute for Competitiveness & Prosperity, Working Paper 10, *Prosperity, inequality, and poverty*, September 2010, 18–19.
2 Economist Michael Hatfield of HRSDC first identified the above-average incidence and the persistence of poverty among a similar list of groups. 'Vulnerability to Persistent Low Income,' Policy Research Institute *Horizons*, 7, no. 2 (2004): 19–26.
3 Institute for Competitiveness & Prosperity, *Prosperity, inequality, and poverty*, 32–3.
4 Ibid., 33–4.
5 Ibid., 40.
6 The program was available to single fathers, but they accounted for only 10 per cent of participants.
7 According to the Participation and Activity Limitation Survey (PALS), part of the Census of Canada; excludes those with 'mild' disability.
8 Martin Prosperity Institute, *Releasing Constraints: Projecting the Economic Impacts of Increased Accessibility in Ontario*, June 2010.
9 Twenty-one per cent of unattached individuals, aged forty-five to sixty-four, have not attained a high school diploma, versus 15 per cent of other Canadians of the same age group; 11 per cent have attained a bachelor's degree versus 15 per cent of other Canadians (2006 Census).
10 Institute for Competitiveness & Prosperity, *Prosperity, Inequality, and Poverty*, 34–5.
11 Ibid., 34–40.
12 Hatfield, 'Vulnerability to Persistent Low Income,' 22.
13 Government of Canada, *Advancing the Inclusion of Persons with Disabilities*, 2005.
14 For example, see Coryse Ciceri and Katherine Scott, 'The Determinants of Employment among Aboriginal Peoples,' in vol. 3 of Jerry P. White et al., eds., *Aboriginal Policy Research: Moving Forward, Making a Difference* (Toronto: Thompson Educational Publishing 2006), 3–32.
15 James Heckman and Dani Rodrik, 'The Productivity Argument for Investing in Young Children,' NBER Working Paper No. 13016 (2007).
16 Miles Corak, 'Do Poor Children Become Poor Adults? Lessons from a

Cross-Country Comparison of Generational Mobility,' Institute for the Study of Labor Markets (2006).

17 Emmanuel Saez and Michael R. Veall, 'The Evolution of High Incomes in Northern America: Lessons from the Canadian Evidence,' *American Economic Review*, 95, no. 3 (2005): 831–49.

18 Institute for Competitiveness & Prosperity, *Prosperity, Inequality, and Poverty*, 23–5.

19 Andrew Sharpe, 'Linkages between Economic Growth and Inequality: An Introduction and Overview,' *Canadian Public Policy*, 29 (2003): S11. Emphasis added.

CREDITS

Exhibit 1: Adapted from the Statistics Canada CANSIM database, http://cansim2.statcan.gc.ca, Table 384–0012, Table 384–0002, Table 510–001, Table 203–0003, Table 203–0010, Table 203–0012, and Table 203–0017 (accessed 7 November 2011); and Statistics Canada, Spending Patterns in Canada, 62–202–X, http://www.statcan.gc.ca/pub/62-202-x/62-202-x2008000-eng.pdf (accessed 7 November 2011). All data have been analyzed by the Authors.

Exhibit 6: Adapted from the Statistics Canada CANSIM database, http://cansim2.statcan.gc.ca, Table 384–0002 and Table 051–0001 (accessed 23 September 2011). All data have been analyzed by the Authors.

Exhibit 9: Adapted from the Statistics Canada CANSIM database, http://cansim2.statcan.gc.ca, Table 282–0012, Table 282–0002, and Table 282–0086 (accessed September 2011). All data have been analyzed by the Authors.

Exhibit 11: Adapted from Statistics Canada, Labour Force Survey, 2006–2010, http://sda.chass.utoronto.ca/sdaweb/html/lfs.htm (accessed June 2011). All data have been analyzed by the Authors.

Exhibit 12: Adapted from Statistics Canada, Labour Force Survey, 2006–2010, http://sda.chass.utoronto.ca/sdaweb/html/lfs.htm (accessed October 2011). All data have been analyzed by the Authors.

Exhibit 16: Adapted from the Statistics Canada CANSIM database, http://cansim2.statcan.gc.ca, Table 384–0002, Table 282–0072, Table 282–0018, and Table 282–0002, Reference years 2004–2009 (accessed 5 October 2011). All data have been analyzed by the Authors.

Exhibit 18: Adapted from the Statistics Canada CANSIM database, http://cansim2.statcan.gc.ca, Table 384–0002, Table 282–0072, Table 282–0018, Table 282–0002, Table 051–0049, and Table 051–0046, Reference years 1996–2009 (accessed 13 October 2011). All data has been analyzed by the Authors.

Exhibit 19: Adapted from Statistics Canada, Census of Canada, 2006, Individuals File (subset compiled from public-use microdata file), using CHASS (distributor), http://sda.chass.utoronto.ca.myaccess.library.utoronto.ca/cgibin/sdacensus/hsda?harcsda+cc06i (accessed 26 November 2008); and Statistics Canada, Business Register Data, 2010. All data have been analyzed by the Authors.

Exhibit 20: Adapted from the Statistics Canada CANSIM database, http://cansim2.statcan.gc.ca, Table 383–0021, Table 379–0025, and Table 282–0008, Reference years 1976–2010 (accessed 10 June 2011). All data have been analyzed by the Authors.

Exhibit 22: Adapted from Statistics Canada, Census of Canada, 1901 – Census of Canada, 2006 (Occupation), using CHASS (distributor), http://sda.chass.utoronto.ca/sdaweb/html/canpumf.htm (accessed December 2008). All data have been analyzed by Kevin Stolarick, Martin Prosperity Institute.

Exhibit 23: Adapted from Statistics Canada, Census of Canada, 2006, Individuals File (subset compiled from public-use microdata file), using CHASS (distributor), http://sda.chass.utoronto.ca.myaccess.library.utoronto.ca/cgi-bin/sdacensus/hsda?harcsda+cc06i (accessed 26 November 2008); and Statistics Canada, Business Register Data, 2006. All data have been analyzed by the Authors.

Exhibit 24: Adapted from Statistics Canada, Census of Canada, 2006, Individuals File (subset compiled from public-use microdata file), using CHASS (distributor), http://sda.chass.utoronto.ca.myaccess.library.utoronto.ca/ cgi-bin/sdacensus/hsda?harcsda+cc06i (accessed 26 November 2008); and Statistics Canada, Business Register Data, 2006. All data have been analyzed by the Authors.

Exhibit 25: Adapted from Statistics Canada, Census of Canada, 2006, Individuals File (subset compiled from public-use microdata file), using CHASS (distributor), http://sda.chass.utoronto.ca.myaccess.library.utoronto.ca/cgi-bin/sdacensus/hsda?harcsda+cc06i (accessed 26 November 2008); Statistics Canada, Business Register Data, 2006; and the Statistics Canada CANSIM database, http://cansim2.statcan.gc.ca, Table 390-0057, Reference year 2005 (accessed 20 April 2008). All data has been analyzed by the Authors.

Exhibit 27: Adapted from Statistics Canada and Council of Ministers of Education, Canada, Education Indicators in Canada: Report of the Pan-Canadian Education Indicators Program, 81–582–XIE, 2005. All data have been analyzed by the Authors.

Exhibit 29: Adapted from the Statistics Canada CANSIM database, http:// cansim2.statcan.gc.ca, Table 385–0001, Reference years 1992–2009 (accessed 1 November 2011). All data have been analyzed by the Authors.

Exhibit 30: Adapted from the Statistics Canada CANSIM database, http:// cansim2.statcan.gc.ca, Table 282–0008, Reference years 1987–2010 (accessed 8 March 2011). All data have been analyzed by the Authors.

Exhibit 36: Adapted from the Statistics Canada CANSIM database, http:// cansim2.statcan.gc.ca, Table 358–0001 and Table 384–0002 (accessed 13 October 2011). All data have been analyzed by the Authors.

Exhibit 38: Adapted from Statistics Canada, Labour Force Survey, 2006–2009, http://sda.chass.utoronto.ca/sdaweb/html/lfs.htm (accessed 16 December 2011). All data have been analyzed by the Authors.

Exhibit 43: Adapted from the Statistics Canada CANSIM database, http://
cansim2.statcan.gc.ca, Table 281–0024 and Table 379–0023; and Statistics
Canada, 2006 Census of Canada (Provinces, Census Divisions, Municipalities),
using CHASS (distributor) http://sda.chass.utoronto.ca/sdaweb/html/can-
pumf.htm (accessed June 2010). All data have been analyzed by the Authors.

Exhibit 44: Adapted from Statistics Canada, 2006 Census of Canada (Provinces, Census Divisions, Municipalities), using CHASS (distributor), http://sda.
chass.utoronto.ca/sdaweb/html/canpumf.htm (accessed September 2010).
All data have been analyzed by the Authors.

Exhibit 45: Adapted from the Statistics Canada CANSIM database, http://
cansim2.statcan.gc.ca, Table 202–0804 and Table 202–0709 (accessed September
2011). All data have been analyzed by the Authors.

Exhibit 46: Adapted from Statistics Canada, 2006 Census of Canada (Provinces, Census Divisions, Municipalities), using CHASS (distributor), http://
sda.chass.utoronto.ca/sdaweb/html/canpumf.htm (accessed September
2011); and Statistics Canada, Participation and Activity Limitation Survey,
2006, using CHASS (distributor), http://sda.chass.utoronto.ca/sdaweb/html/
health.htm (accessed September 2011). All data have been analyzed by the
Authors.

Exhibit A: Adapted from Statistics Canada, Labour Force Survey, 2009
(accessed 16 December 2010). All data have been analyzed by the Authors.

INDEX

Patriot Forge Co., 77
Peron, Juan, 31
physical resources: and competitiveness, 15–16; investment in, 104–8;
and rivalry, 21; and value added,
17. *See also* manufacturing
Poland, 148
Porter, Michael, 6, 23, 63–4, 74
Portugal, 148
Potash Corporation, 155, 157
poverty: cyclical nature of, 177–8;
high-risk groups, 175–7, 176, 178–
81; Low-Income Cut-Off (LICO),
176–8; and Marginal Effective Tax
Rates (METRs), 113, 117–22, 200;
measure of, 176, 177; minimum
wages, 191; and public policy,
180, 192–3, 197. *See also* income;
unemployment
pressure, 93–4, 143, 162–3
Principles of Scientific Management
(Taylor), 147
Procter & Gamble (P&G), 136–7
product development, 140–1
productivity: in Canada, 6–7, 62; and
clustered industries, 74–6; and
competitiveness, 23, 63–4; as concept, 52–3; country comparisons,
53–5; defined, 5; drivers of, 65–7;
and economic growth, 61–3; and
education, 99–100; and efficiency,
59–60; and global leaders, 151–2;
and innovation, 53, 55–8, 59–60;
labour productivity, 17; limits on,
58–60; and manufacturing, 77–9;
and prosperity gap, 64; and trade,
163–4; and urbanization, 71–3; and
value added, 19
productivity gap: attitudes toward,
85; in Canada, 4–5; and invest-

ment, 105–6, 108; and urbanization, 72–3; and utilization, 34. *See
also* United States
profile, 34, 35–6, 38
prosperity: in Canada, 27–9; and
competitiveness, 26–7; country
comparisons, 53–5; defined, 24–6;
distribution of, 189–92; factors of,
33–4; measurement of, 17; and
productivity, 62; sources of, 31;
and trade, 159–61. *See also* economic outlook
prosperity gap: and competitiveness,
30–1; and disabled persons, 185;
and GDP, 28–9; and intensity gap,
47; and productivity, 64; recommendations on, 8–9, 194–5; and
standard of living, 7–8; as term, 4;
and work effort, 47–8, 50
protectionism, 171–3
public policy: and foreign takeovers,
152–3, 155–8; and innovation, 128,
131–4, 134–5, 195; and investment,
96–8, 146; and low-income Canadians, 200; and poverty, 180, 192–
3, 197; priorities of, 7, 30, 195–6;
and taxation, 135; and urbanization, 70; and venture capital,
138. *See also* health care; social
programs
pulp and paper industry, 21

Quebec, 172

reciprocity, 156–7
R & D: investment in, 134; need for,
6, 7; and public policy, 131; and
risk, 85–6. *See also* innovation
Regent Park, 183
regional disparities, 40, 42